Just As I Am:
MARRIED, DIVORCED AND REMARRIED!

WAYNE DUNAWAY

xulon
PRESS

PREFACE

Just as I am without one plea,
But that thy blood was shed for me,
And that thou bidst me come to thee,
O Lamb of God, I come, I come.

These are words from one of the most familiar Christian hymns of all time. It was written by Charlotte Elliott in 1834 and has been sung countless times through the years by those whose hearts are set on seeking God. It is still being sung today. These are words cherished by all of us who have come to Jesus for salvation. We came to rid our souls of "one dark blot, to Him whose blood can cleanse each spot." We have learned that His love breaks "every barrier down" including those barriers created by guilt from failed marriages. I speak of those who have been married, divorced, and remarried. Those who have been in marriages that did not work out, for whatever reason, and have started over in a new relationship. The words of "Just As I Am" apply to you, too. Just like the rest of us — sinners — you, too, can come to Jesus: *Just as I am* — married, divorced, and remarried.

This book sets forth what I believe the Bible teaches on the subject of marriage, divorce, and remarriage. It is the result of my own personal study of the subject over the last forty years. I have studied it periodically all of my preaching life and have read numerous books, articles, and sermons on the subject as well as listened to many tapes and lectures. I have obviously changed my mind about some aspects of the subject based on continual learning and study, as I have on numerous other subjects. Like most preachers, I believed what I was taught without question at first, and then over the years began to study and think for myself about this and many other subjects. I have concluded that some of the things I was taught and that I once believed are simply not true.

I can say that I have never refused to baptize anyone who confessed faith in Jesus and I have never been involved in breaking up any families of those who have been divorced and remarried. One of the first books I read on the subject when I first started preaching was a book titled, *The Sermon On The Mount and the Civil State*, by Foy E. Wallace, Jr. His writings influenced me greatly in the beginning of my preaching career and he was totally opposed to breaking up homes and meddling in the marital affairs of others. This is not to say that I did not make a lot of mistakes in dealing with others, but I can say that breaking up established families or refusing to baptize divorced and remarried believers was not among them.

I will primarily use the New King James Version of the Bible in this book because it is the translation with which I am most familiar. It and the King James Version have been my primary study Bibles for over forty-four years. I may refer to others, but anything I believe on the subject of marriage, divorce, and remarriage, I will be able to prove from simply reading the New King James Version of the Bible.

I will use a question and answer format in the book in order to make what is being taught simple and easy to understand. I will answer each question as thoroughly, yet as briefly, as I can. I will try to use questions that will help us understand the overall teaching of the Bible as well as certain specific passages that deal with the subject. I will also use the letters MDR throughout the book to refer to marriage, divorce and remarriage for the sake of brevity.

I realize at the outset that this is a highly controversial and emotional subject and one that I believe has been misunderstood by many of those in the Restoration Movement as well as in the religious world at large. When you speak about divorce and remarriage you press a spiritual "hot button" among believers in many cases. But it seems to me that some of those who preach the most about it seem to know the least concerning what the Bible actually says. It is my judgment, based on what I have read and heard from others, that very few have actually studied what the Bible really teaches about it. As with most subjects the majority of people and preachers I know simply repeat what they have heard and have been taught by others. I have done that myself on any number of topics (including certain aspects of this one) and, therefore, I completely understand how that can happen to any of us. I also realize that many who read this book will not agree with the answers and conclusions given and that is fine. I do not agree with many of the positions I have read and that is why I am writing this book. So I do not take offense if someone disagrees with the views I hold on the subject of marriage, divorce, and remarriage. This is simply what I believe and I have written it down for others to consider in light of the Bible. Hopefully, you will find enough good things that will be helpful to you and will make it worthwhile to read the book even if you do not agree with all of the conclusions.

If you have been divorced and remarried, I do encourage you to study the conclusions in the book before you give up on Christ and the church. Divorce is sometimes an option and, sadly, in some cases it is the *only* option. For one to teach that we can divorce our faithful mates for just any and every cause is sinful. But on the other hand, for someone else to teach that one must remain in an abusive marriage filled with domestic violence, or remain in a marriage that causes one to be unfaithful to Jesus, or else that person must remain single for the rest of their lives is, in my judgment, both cruel and heartless. **Furthermore, breaking up established families whose marital status does not measure up to some preacher or elder's opinions or views is not necessarily God's plan or purpose.** Please rest assured that God is not responsible for the false ideas and apparent unmerciful attitudes displayed by some preachers and other believers. I personally believe that in most cases the majority of them are honest brethren who are simply saying what they have been taught by others and simply do not know the real facts. But the destructive results and broken homes or the MDR people who are turned away from the grace and mercy of Jesus because they rightly refuse to divorce their present faithful mates because of the unfounded theories and human opinions of religious leaders should not go unchallenged.

This book will most likely give many of you an alternative view of what God's word actually teaches about MDR from those you may have heard and been taught in the past. Whether we agree or not is not that important to me, but what God has said is important. We all should be open and honest enough to let those who are personally involved in MDR to make up their own minds based on all of the Biblical evidence that is available rather than seeking to make those decisions for them on these highly controversial matters that have such serious and eternal consequences. This is one reason I am writing and publishing this book. I am not trying to "make friends and influence people" to like me as a person or a preacher, as this is not a subject that will contribute to that in many cases. But I am trying to be true and honest about what I personally believe that the Bible teaches on this very important matter, having studied it off and on for over forty years. I am also trying to help those involved in MDR to understand that what God actually teaches about it is both reasonable and right when all of the facts are known. God is merciful to all, including those who have made bad marriage decisions. He wants us all to be saved and, hopefully, this book will prove it. Jesus came that we might have an abundant life now and eternal life in heaven—and that includes forgiveness for fornicators, idolaters, drunkards, adulterers, murderers, liars and all others who diligently seek Him. "And such were some of you" applies to all churches, not just Corinth. Any of us (including those guilty of marital sins) can be washed, sanctified and justified by the cleansing power of Jesus and the Spirit of God (1 Cor. 6:9-11). If you have been divorced and have since remarried then hopefully, when you finish the book, you will have a greater appreciation of the words, "Just as I am without one plea but that thy blood was shed for me…O Lamb of God, I come, I come!"

Finally, Paul had a good plan for Timothy in 2 Timothy 2:7 and one that I will leave with you as you begin to read this book: *"Consider what I say, and may the Lord give you understanding in all things"*

Wayne Dunaway
November 2014

DEDICATION

This book is dedicated to those who have been married, divorced and remarried and have come to Jesus for salvation (as well as to those who may want to come to Jesus and be saved). Some of you have suffered enough guilt, rejection and/or suspicion because your marriage did not work out and so you have started over. It is time for healing. It is time to focus on God's grace, mercy and peace. It is time to "rejoice in the Lord and again I say rejoice" (Phil. 4:4). You may not be able to regain some of the things you have lost, but you can rejoice "in the Lord"—always. If you are "in Christ," all of your sins are forgiven and this includes marital mistakes or sins against a mate. It is now time to move on. We should all *learn* from the past, but never *live* in the past. As Christians, we have a *new heart* for a *new start*. There is a *new birth* for *those on earth* and if you have not experienced it, you can. This is true no matter what your current marital state is. You can reach out to Jesus and be saved in spite of the fact that you may be in a second or subsequent marriage.

Prejudice has always been a problem in the church and still is. When I first became a Christian back in 1970, racism had been practiced as a way of life in many of our churches— even to the point of some elders standing in a door to keep those of other races from coming in. *Other churches allowed them in but had "designated places" for them to sit and treated them as second-class citizens in the kingdom.* There were most likely some of us in those days who simply misunderstood what the Bible taught about it, perhaps others of us refused to really study the issue for fear of where it might lead, and some of us may have simply denied what the Bible clearly said. But the results were the same. And while we have, with God's help, made tremendous progress in these areas, we still have a long way to go. But progress has been and is being made and that is a good thing.

The same is true concerning those who have been married, divorced and remarried. The church has practiced discrimination in the past and in too many churches it is still practiced today concerning those who have been married more than once. **And while as far I know none of us have literally stood in the door of the building to keep them out, many have been turned away from the kingdom because of demands that God never made or, if they were baptized, they were/are treated as second class citizens in the kingdom.** As in the case of racism and other issues, I am sure that some do so as a matter of conviction because of a misunderstanding of what the Bible teaches about it, others possibly refuse to really study the subject for fear of where it might lead or how brethren may react, and others seem bent on simply continuing to demand breaking up established families and demanding that those involved in MDR divorce their present faithful mates which is in itself sinful. I have to believe that in the large majority of cases it is not necessarily a matter of honesty and integrity, but rather misinterpreting and misunderstanding what the Bible actually says. But the view that many in our churches hold about MDR is simply not true, regardless of who teaches it, how many believe it, or how long it has been taught.

What does the Bible really teach about marriage, divorce and remarriage? This book will reveal what I personally believe the Bible teaches about it and will explain the reasons why I am firmly convinced that what I believe is true. It seems to me that the Bible is very clear on this subject if we let it interpret itself, and, hopefully, you will see that too. God bless you for turning to Jesus for forgiveness and I wish for you a greater understanding of and appreciation for God's *goodness, grace* and *guidance*. When you finish reading the book, I hope you can say that it has contributed to your peace of mind and renewed assurance. My prayer is that you will know that Jesus, the great "I AM," accepts us just as we are—even if we are "married, divorced and remarried."

Wayne Dunaway
November 2014

TABLE OF CONTENTS

1

WHY AM I WRITING
THIS BOOK?

1. "The preacher where I attend Church said that my husband
and I had to divorce after eighteen years of marriage. We love
each other dearly and we have two teenage children. I called
another preacher and he too said we had to divorce. Is that
really what the Bible teaches? Both preachers indicated that
we were 'living in adultery' because we are both 'still married' to the ones we 'divorced' because according to them
our divorces were not "scriptural!" Can that possibly be true?
Do we really have to divorce and live separately and single
for the rest of our lives and leave our children with only one
parent in the home in order to go to heaven?"

This is the gist of what the lady said to me on the phone.

I had never met her before and I had no idea what kind of
condition she was in, but she sounded devastated. I told her
that I did not believe that the Bible taught any such thing
and that I believe it would be wrong for her to divorce her

husband. I told her I would come over and talk to her and her husband and we would read what the Bible said about it.

I will never forget walking into their house. It was as if someone had died suddenly and they could not believe it. They were completely shocked and devastated. They could not believe that they were put in that situation and given that ultimatum. The husband showed me some verses that the preacher had given him where the Bible demands that people repent of their sins (including Acts 2:38 and 17:30) and said the preacher had told them they had to divorce and could no longer live together as husband and wife after being happily married for over eighteen years! The husband had been teaching a class at church and his wife was very active in all that was going on. But now they must divorce, leaving the children with only one parent in the home, and they must both remain single for the rest of their lives or be lost—all because of something that happened over eighteen years earlier! Is this really what Jesus teaches? Were those preachers right in telling them to divorce each other after eighteen years of love, devotion and faithfulness to each other in their marriage relationship? My answer was and is, "Absolutely not!" **It would be sinful to do what those preachers said! It is treacherous! Divorcing a faithful spouse is condemned in no uncertain terms in both the Old Testament and the New.** *Demanding* **that a married couple divorce is even worse!**

2. This is the main reason I have chosen to write and publish this book! This couple is just one among many who have been married, divorced, and are now remarried. They have come to Jesus and the church for salvation, strength

and security only to be met in some churches with rebuke, ridicule and rejection. There is no good news in this kind of disastrous message and there is nothing in the Bible that requires any such drastic measures. *Foy Wallace, Jr. in his book on the "The Sermon On The Mount and the Civil State" called it a "presumptuous procedure," but I would call it a "preposterous practice."* It is serious business to demand something that God hates (Mal. 2:16). It is serious, serious business to seek to break up established families and leave children without one of their parents in the home all because of the unfounded and unscriptural opinions of men.

3. Hopefully, when you finish the book, you will see how God's word deals with those who are involved in MDR and how His grace and mercy applies in those situations. There are plenty of churches loyal to New Testament Christianity that do not hold this view of MDR and our numbers are growing as more and more preachers and churches are studying the subject for themselves.

4. We forgive fornicators, prostitutes, drunkards, child molesters, murderers, thieves, liars, adulterers, drug addicts, dope dealers, sex offenders and such like. They can repent and turn to Jesus and go on with their lives with their wives/husbands and children if they have them—unless, unless, unless they have made a marriage mistake themselves or married the wrong person in the past. In that case, they cannot go on with their wives/husbands and children. In those cases, according to some (and, again, their numbers are steadily shrinking), they must divorce their mates and live single for the rest of their lives *even if they were deserted and/or physically abused and/or unjustly divorced by a marriage partner*

in the past. If anyone actually thinks that that sounds like the Jesus we read about in the Bible, then they do not know the Jesus that we know and quite obviously don't know what the Bible teaches on this subject, at least in my judgment!

5. The rest of this book is dedicated to proving that God is merciful to those who have made bad marriage decisions or those who have sinned against marriage in the past and want to be saved in spite of the fact that they are now in second or subsequent marriages.

6. The message of the cross is: *Just as I am...married, divorced and remarried!*

2

WHAT IS GOD'S ORIGINAL PLAN FOR MARRIAGE?

1. As we begin this series of questions about MDR, it is important to understand that marriage originated in the mind of a loving and concerned God for the good and happiness of both man and woman. It did not originate in the mind of Satan. It did not even originate in the mind of man. It came from God. It was God who said, "*It is not good that man be alone.*" Everything God made in the beginning was good except one—a bachelor. It was God who said, "*I will make him a helper comparable to him.*" It was God who made a woman from one of Adam's ribs and *"brought her to the man."* (Gen. 2:18-22). And it was God who inspired the following words: "*Therefore a man shall leave his father and mother and be joined to his wife, and they shall become one flesh.*" (Gen. 2:24)

2. Marriage then is God's plan and provision for both the male and female that He created. God is the one who decided that men and women should be married. **God's original plan was for one man and one woman to be "one flesh" for life.**

His ideal will for marriage has never changed at any time.
Jesus reaffirmed God's original plan in Matthew 19:4-6 with
the following words:

> *And He answered and said to them, "Have you
> not read that He who made them at the begin-
> ning 'made them male and female,' and said,
> 'For this reason a man shall leave his father
> and mother and be joined to his wife, and the
> two shall become one flesh'? So then, they are
> no longer two but one flesh. Therefore what
> God has joined together, let not man separate."*

3. The Bible teaches that marriage is honorable in all (Heb.
13:4). It is God's way to satisfy the social, sexual, and spiritual needs of men and women. Therefore, I want to encourage
all married couples to make marriage the best it can be.
Marriage demands our very best efforts. Marriage calls for
a lot of compromises as well as a great deal of patience and
understanding. But a successful marriage has been called
"heaven on earth" and it can be. It is worth every effort we
put into it to make it happen. I hope and pray that it will be
that way for all married couples who read this book. Since
God Himself ordained and sanctified the marriage relationship, then I want to encourage all married couples to do as
the Bible teaches in Proverbs 3:5-7: *"Trust in the Lord with
all your heart, and lean not on your own understanding; In
all your ways acknowledge Him, And He shall direct your
paths."* God wants to direct our paths, not only in our personal lives, but more importantly, for our present study, in
our marriages.

4. God joins couples together when they follow His instructions and they become "one flesh." He joins those who leave father and mother and cleave to each other. God joins those who sincerely commit their lives to each other as companions for life. This is the marriage covenant. Those whom God joins are not to separate or divorce. This is His ideal will and His original plan for all marriages for all time. It has always been His ideal will and original plan.

5. **Nine of God's moral laws recorded in the "Ten Commandments" have never changed since the beginning of time.** Moses revealed them but he did not create them. They did not begin when God spoke them to the children of Israel and they did not end with the death of Jesus on the cross. It has never been right to have other gods before Him. It has never been right to bear false witness or lie. It has never been right to murder or steal. It has never been right to covet a neighbor's wife or commit adultery.

6. The same is true with God's original plan for marriage. It has always been, and still is, God's will and plan that there be one man for one woman committed to each other for life. He never wanted or intended for husbands and wives to separate or divorce (Matt. 19:4-6). He has always wanted *"every man to have his own wife, and every woman to have her own husband"* (1 Cor. 7:2). He has always desired that they be companions until death (Rom. 7:4).

7. Nothing that is written in this book should be interpreted as encouraging or endorsing the breaking of the marriage covenant with a faithful spouse. Divorcing a faithful spouse is always wrong, no matter who does it. God has always

"hated" divorcing faithful companions and those who do so sin, not only against their mate, but more importantly against their Maker!

8. Keep this in mind throughout the rest of this book. There is nothing that will change what God has always wanted and intended concerning husbands and wives in the marriage covenant. It has always been and will always be, *"What therefore God has joined together, let not man separate."*

9. In fact, I will state the following *disclaimer* here at the beginning of the book, so that there will be no misunderstanding concerning what I believe about the subject (and yes I will repeat myself for the sake of emphasis): *Nothing that is written in this book should be interpreted as encouraging or endorsing the breaking of the marriage covenant with a faithful spouse. This book is primarily about pardon for those who have sinned, and not about permission for those who want to sin. It is about forgiveness of sin, and not about freedom to sin. Divorcing a faithful spouse, especially in order to marry someone else, is always wrong no matter who does it. God has always "hated" divorcing faithful companions and those who do so sin, not only against their mate but more importantly against their Maker! Divorcing a faithful mate in order to marry someone else is sinful, period. In doing so, one "commits adultery" against the faithful spouse (Mk. 10:11). It is treacherous! It is faithless. It is condemned in no uncertain terms both in the Old Testament and the New (Malachi 2:13-16; Matthew 19:1-9). If you are now married to a faithful spouse (whether first, second, or fifth) God says that you are to stay married. Do not divorce the faithful mate you are married to*

even if preachers or others say it can or should be done!!! In fact, if you are now married and are having problems in your marriage I suggest you stop reading this book now and go to a marriage counselor or some other qualified source and save your marriage, especially if children are involved. All divorces have negative consequences and need to be avoided at all costs if possible. In many cases most of the marital issues can be solved with the proper help and determination. Marital problems can even make the marriage stronger and better in the long run. Even marital failures do not have to be fatal or final if we can learn to face them with faith, forgiveness and focusing on the future. The message of the Bible and this book is that what God has joined together let not man separate. If you are married "stay married" if possible! Make every effort to make it work because that is God's way and the best way for all concerned.

10. With these thoughts clearly in mind, we move forward in our study.

3

WHAT IS MARRIAGE?

1. Marriage, according to the Bible, is a "covenant" between a man and a woman. It is an agreement to be companions for life. It is two people becoming "one flesh" or fusing/combining/ blending their hearts and lives together as one unit.

2. We must understand what marriage is in order to understand anything taught about it. This point needs to be clear in our minds as we begin the study concerning what the Bible teaches on this very important matter. We are husband and wife "by covenant." Malachi makes that abundantly clear when he says: *"Yet she is your companion. And your wife by covenant"* (2:14)

3. A covenant is a "formal agreement" between two people. It is a pledge or promise or vow of allegiance to each other to be companions for life. **Marriage is a commitment to each other to be companions *for* each other, *to* each other, and *with* each other.**

4. Malachi says that your wife is your companion: *"Yet she is your companion. And your wife by covenant."* The covenant of

marriage, then, is an agreement and pledge to be a "partner" — helper, companion — and when one breaks that agreement and pledge, they have broken the marriage covenant. Nothing could be simpler, yet nothing, it seems, is more misunderstood than this one point when it comes to MDR. There are many Christian writers and teachers with whom I am familiar who claim to have "all the answers" concerning who is entitled to be married and who is not, who cannot even agree among themselves concerning what constitutes a marriage. What is marriage? That is a question that deserves and demands a simple and straightforward, definite answer. And yet, when one asks that question, he or she may find that the one doing so much teaching on MDR cannot give a biblical answer to the question. If we do not even understand what constitutes a marriage, indeed, what marriage itself is, then we certainly cannot responsibly study all the details about when a marriage ends or what to do when a marriage covenant fails or especially who is indeed married and who is not.

5. A mate is a "companion." When God created Eve for Adam it was because it was not good for man to be "alone." He needed a companion suitable for his emotional, physical, and spiritual needs. Husbands and wives need each other to make life complete as God intended.

6. Yes, this is the simple answer. This is the straightforward answer. This is the Biblical answer. What is marriage? It is a covenant agreement between two people to fulfill the emotional, physical and spiritual needs that marriage is designed to provide for each other. It has been that way since the Garden of Eden and it has never changed.

4

WHAT "CEREMONY" IS INVOLVED IN BECOMING MARRIED?

1. What kind of "ceremony" does the Bible require for two people to be joined in marriage? The only answer that could be given to this question is: Whatever ceremony (or lack thereof) or custom is in effect at the time that makes two people "married" in the society in which they live is what constitutes a marriage ceremony. A ceremony does not necessarily make a marriage as God intended unless the two involved are really committed to each other, but it is part of the civil law as well as a part of the marriage covenant.

2. Isaac took Rebekah into his mother's tent and she became his wife. In that day and in that culture she could become "his wife" in the tent. A *private commitment* between the two was evidently the custom of getting married at the time.

> *Then Isaac brought her into his mother Sarah's tent; and he took Rebekah and she became his wife, and he loved her. So Isaac was comforted after his mother's death.* (Gen. 24:67).

3. Jesus went to a wedding in Cana of Galilee where He turned water into wine for the wedding guests. In this case there was obviously some kind of "wedding ceremony" as in our own western culture of this day and time.

"On the third day there was a wedding in Cana of Galilee, and the mother of Jesus was there. Now both Jesus and His disciples were invited to the wedding" (John 2:1-2).

4. Some have been married by "jumping the broom," others have had formal ceremonies of some sort, and there are other ways of entering a marital covenant. In our country, we can go to the courthouse, get married in a church building, at home, on the lake, or anywhere else we choose, by anyone appointed to perform marriage ceremonies. In some states there are "Common Law" marriages where couples simply agree to be married. But whatever the civil ceremony or custom of the time is, as it relates to marriage, is what constitutes a legal marriage covenant.

5. **It is the "marriage covenant" with each other that constitutes marriage wherever, however, and whenever that "covenant" (commitment/agreement) is made.** Throughout this study we must keep in mind that Malachi 2:14 says, *"she is your wife by covenant."*

6. The "Marriage Ceremony" is simply a formal expression and finalizing of the commitment made by the couple involved. In our country, in most cases, a man and woman commit to each other and enter a covenant with each other privately before the marriage ceremony takes place. This commitment to each other to live together as companions is

the covenant God had in mind from the beginning and it has never changed. How we finalize the commitment varies, but it is the *commitment* or *covenant* we make with each other that makes a marriage a marriage.

7. The Bible simply does not prescribe any certain ceremony or formalities that must take place to make a marriage a marriage.

5

WHAT DOES SEX HAVE TO DO WITH BEING MARRIED?

1. Sex has *nothing* to do with whether or not a couple is married. This is one of the most misunderstood and overlooked points concerning the Bible's teaching on marriage. If people would understand this one simple truth, much confusion and error regarding the subject of MDR would be cleared up immediately.

2. Sex is not part of the "marriage covenant." **Sex is a privilege of those who have already entered the "marriage covenant" or those who have pledged themselves to one another as marriage companions for life, but the sex act itself has nothing to do with whether we are married or not.** Again, this is one of the most important things to remember and constantly keep in mind when studying the subject of MDR.

3. For example, a couple too old for sex can still get married. They can still enter a marriage "covenant." A couple who are physically incapable of having sex for whatever

reason (age, injury, physical disability) could still agree to get married and be companions socially and spiritually in a marriage "covenant." Joseph was married to Mary months before they had sex.

> *Then Joseph, being aroused from sleep, did as the angel of the Lord commanded him and took to him his wife, and **did not know her** till she had brought forth her firstborn Son* (Matt. 1:24-25).

Observe carefully that even though Mary was his wife, he did not "know her" sexually until after Jesus was born.

4. When a man and a woman stand before me as an ordained minister of the gospel and I pronounce them "husband and wife" they are married at that point. They are not "almost" married, "nearly" married, "somewhat" married, or in the "process" of getting married. They are married then and there.

5. Some believe that the sex act "consummates" or completes a marriage covenant. They believe that the sex act puts the "finishing touch" on a marriage relationship. But if a couple is not already married when they first have sex, then it is called "*fornication*" in the Bible, not *consummation*.

6. The very idea that a couple is not actually married at the time they are pronounced husband and wife in our country would be hilarious if it were not so serious. I mean no one would know it! Everybody involved would think they were married. No one! No not one! Nobody would think or act as though they were just in the "process" of getting married. The minister would indicate, and everyone involved

including the bride and groom, would believe that when they are pronounced "husband and wife" they are married then and there. And guess what? They are!

7. In 1 Corinthians 7:2, Paul said that the way to "avoid fornication" is for a man to have a wife. He is not to fornicate in order to get one. It is "wife" first, then the sex. For one to "avoid" fornication, a man needs to have sex with one who is already his "wife," before the sexual activity begins.

8. Furthermore, if couples are not actually married when they are pronounced "husband and wife" then there is a lot of misunderstanding, deception, or, maybe in some cases, outright lies being told at the time. I, personally, would have no part of such a facade. As a minister, if I did not believe that they were actually married, I would not say, imply, or even insinuate that they were. I would simply say that they are in the "process" of getting married or whatever I really believed about it. I would not pronounce them "husband and wife" if there was something else that they had to do to be married—like *consummate, fornicate,* or go on a *date*.

9. Remember this: **If they are married in the ceremony, then they are not married in the bed. But if they are married in the bed, then they are not married in the ceremony**.

Note: For more on this point see Appendix number one: WHAT IS WRONG WITH TEACHING THAT THE MARRIAGE IS CONSUMMATED BY THE "SEXUAL UNION"?

6

What Is Meant By "The Two Shall Be One Flesh"?

1. A married couple becoming "one flesh" refers to the "joining" of their "spirits" (hearts) in marriage. It is two people becoming "one flesh" or fusing/combining their hearts and lives together as *one family unit*. It involves "joining" of "spirits" in commitment and companionship. It is this joining that one is not to put asunder or separate. Jesus made that abundantly clear when He said:

> *For this reason a man shall leave his father and mother and be joined to his wife, and the two shall become one flesh'? So then, they are no longer two but* **one flesh***. Therefore what God has joined together, let not man separate."* (Matt. 19:5-6).

2. Becoming "one flesh" does not refer to the sex act in marriage, even though the sex act is an "expression" of the "one flesh" relationship that a husband and wife already enjoy before they engage in sex. Sex with a marriage partner is

an "expression" of the "one flesh" relationship, but it is not the relationship itself nor does it "consummate" it. Sex is a privilege for those who are married, but it does not produce a marriage. I am "one flesh" with my wife whether we are having sex or not. I will still be "one flesh" with my wife if we both live long enough and stop having sex.

3. A couple with no interest in sex due to age, disability, or some other factor, can get married and be in a "one flesh" relationship without ever having sex.

4. Jesus made it clear that becoming "one flesh" is being "joined together" in marriage. Read it again:

> *For this reason a man shall leave his father and mother and **be joined** to his wife, and the two shall become one flesh'? So then, they are no longer two but **one flesh**. Therefore what God has joined together, let not man separate."* (Matt. 19:5-6).

5. Observe that Jesus said that a man who is "joined" to his wife is "one flesh" with her. It is the "leaving" parents and being "joined" to his wife that makes them "one flesh."

6. Furthermore, Jesus said the "two" shall be "one flesh." Then He said, "Therefore" (that is, because the two are one flesh) they are "joined together" (whether having sex or not) and man is not to "separate" the "two." But if this refers to the sex act, then the husband and the wife are both guilty of "separating" the "one flesh" relationship when they finish having sex. If not, why not?

7. If we "cleave" we are "one flesh," but if we "leave" we put asunder what God has "joined." Therefore, "one flesh" is a joining of "spirits/hearts" in a marriage relationship.

8. The "one flesh" relationship in marriage is when two individuals become united into one in purposing, pledging, and promising to be marriage companions for life. The two are united into one in commitment, love, and companionship which forms *one family unit*.

9. In Ephesians 5:22-32, Paul uses the marital relationship of the husband and wife to illustrate the relationship of Christ and the church.

> *Wives, submit to your own husbands, as to the Lord. For the husband is head of the wife, as also Christ is head of the church; and He is the Savior of the body. Therefore, just as the church is subject to Christ, so let the wives be to their own husbands in everything. Husbands, love your wives, just as Christ also loved the church and gave Himself for her, that He might sanctify and cleanse her with the washing of water by the word, that He might present her to Himself a glorious church, not having spot or wrinkle or any such thing, but that she should be holy and without blemish. So husbands ought to love their own wives as their own bodies; he who loves his wife loves himself. For no one ever hated his own flesh, but nourishes and cherishes it, just as the Lord does the church. For we are members of His body, of His flesh and of His*

*bones. "For this reason a man shall leave his father and mother and be joined to his wife, and **the two shall become one flesh.**" This is a great mystery, but **I speak concerning Christ and the church.** Nevertheless let each one of you in particular so love his own wife as himself, and let the wife see that she respects her husband.*

10. Notice that Paul refers to the statement recorded in Genesis 2:24 and Matthew 19:5 concerning *"the two shall become one flesh,"* and applies it to *"Christ and the church."* It is interesting that nothing in Ephesians 5:22-32 is said about sex. It is all about commitment, respect, love, nourishing, and cherishing—nothing about sex. Why? **It is because sex in marriage is an expression of the "one flesh" relationship, but it is not the relationship itself.**

11. Just answer the following questions in your own mind. The answers will help you realize that becoming "one flesh" with a spouse does not refer to having sex with a spouse.

When a husband is not having sex with his wife, is he still "one flesh" at that time?

Is he only "one flesh" with his wife during sex? If so, when sex is over has he put asunder or separated the "one flesh" relationship?

If a married couple gets too old for sex, do they cease to be "one flesh"?

When God refers to "leaving" and "joining" was He talking about leaving one relationship and entering (joining) another relationship? Or was He talking about leaving a relationship with his parents and simply having sex with his wife?

Did being "joined to his wife" and becoming "one flesh" mean the same thing? If not, what is the difference?

If Jesus and Paul were referring exclusively or even primarily to sex by their reference to "one flesh," does the Bible teach anywhere that the "sex act" has that much power? If so, where does it teach that?

If Jesus and Paul were referring to the sex act, why would a person not be married to every one they had sex with? They would be "one flesh." Since, according to some, the "sex act" makes a man "one flesh," and the "one flesh" relationship causes a man to "be joined to his wife," why wouldn't a man be married to every woman with whom he had sex?

12. Let me repeat myself because of the importance of this vital point: Sex has nothing to do with whether or not a couple is married. Sex is a privilege for those who are married. Marriage is a covenant or agreement or vow or promise or commitment to be "companions" for life. **Marriage is a "Covenant Relationship" and not a sexual experience.** Being "one flesh" refers to two people fusing/combining their hearts and lives together as one *family unit*. Becoming "one flesh" occurs in *sincere hearts* and not in *sexual heat*.

Note: For more on this point see Appendix number two: IF "ONE FLESH" DOES NOT REFER TO THE SEX ACT, WHAT DOES FIRST CORINTHIANS 6:16-17 MEAN?

7

HOW DOES GOD JOIN A COUPLE IN MARRIAGE?

1. What part does God have in a marriage covenant? The Bible teaches that "God" is the one who "joins" a couple in marriage. Jesus makes that clear in the following statement on the subject:

> And He answered and said to them, "Have you not read that He who made them at the beginning 'made them male and female,' and said, 'For this reason a man shall leave his father and mother and be joined to his wife, and the two shall become one flesh'? So then, they are no longer two but one flesh. Therefore what **God has joined** together, let not man separate." (Matt. 19:4-6).

2. Observe that "*God has joined together*" those who "leave" parents and are united with each other. It is the man who is "joined to his wife" that "God has joined" together with his wife. God does not join together any who do not decide in

their own minds to be joined together. It is the husband and wife who are married. It is not the husband, wife, and God who are joined together. It is the "two" who become "one flesh," not the "three." When two atheists marry, God joins them together—even though He, most likely, is not even invited to the wedding.

3. The question then is: How does God "join" a couple together? Most all agree that "God joins" a couple together, but how?

4. It is important to understand that marriage is not a "church ordinance" or "church sacrament." Marriage existed long before the church was established. This means that the church has nothing to do with whether a couple is married or not. Those in and out of the church are "joined" in marriage by God when they enter the marriage covenant with each other. **The view held by some good brethren that those in the world are not subject to the Lord's marriage law is simply not true.**

5. It is also important to understand in what sense God is said to join two people together in marriage. Observe the following three points on how God joins a couple in marriages.

6. *First*, God "joins" a couple together because He *ordained marriage* in the beginning. Marriage originated in the mind of God. Marriage is a divine institution.

> And the LORD **God said**, *"It is not good that man should be alone; I will make him a helper comparable to him."* (Gen. 2:18).

7. *Second*, God "joins" a couple together because He is the one who *gives the qualifications* for marriage. He said that they must be "male and female." He said that they were to "leave father and mother" and hold fast to each other. He said the two will be united into a single entity. He said they would live together with one purpose and be one family unit (one flesh).

> *And He answered and said to them, "Have you not read that He who made them at the beginning 'made them **male** and **female**,' and said, 'For this reason a man shall leave his father and mother and be joined to his wife, and the **two shall become one flesh'**?* (Matt. 19:4-5).

8. *Third*, God "joins" a couple together because He is a *witness* to the covenant that they make with each other.

> *Because the Lord has been **witness** between you and the wife of your youth, with whom you have dealt treacherously; yet she is your companion and your wife by covenant.* (Mal. 2:14).

9. This is the sense in which God joins a couple together in marriage and it is never, never, never against their wills. They must decide to "be joined" together before God can join them together. So we need to understand that God does not "join" a couple with some "mysterious clamp" or in some "mystical way" that does not involve the "wills" of the ones who are married. The one who leaves his parents and "holds fast" (ESV) to his wife is the one God "joins." If a couple does not decide to "leave" and "cleave," then there is no

reason to believe that God joins them together. There is no "mysterious magnet" that God uses to draw them together or make them marry against their wills. God is not the author of "shotgun" weddings.

10. It is the same way with divorce. If a couple decides not to stay joined together then God does not have some "invisible clamp" or "mystical magnet" that holds them together against their wills. If a husband or wife (or both) later decides to leave the marriage relationship, God will know that the relationship is "asunder." Even though God may not approve, He does acknowledge that they are separated/divorced. *It will all ride on what they decide.*

11. It seems to me that God "joins" couples in marriage in much the same way as the "Holy Spirit" makes elders in the church.

> *Therefore take heed to yourselves and to all the flock, among which* **the Holy Spirit has made you overseers,** *to shepherd the church of God which He purchased with His own blood.* (Acts 20:28).

12. Observe that the Holy Spirit "made" them overseers. But how did the Holy Spirit make them overseers? The Holy Spirit ordained the office, gave the qualifications, gifted the men for the work, described the work, etc. But being an elder or not being an elder is the decision of the one involved and the congregation where he is involved. And either one (the congregation or the elder himself) can "unmake" what the

Holy Spirit made if they decide to do it (whether they are right or wrong in their decision).

13. The same is true with the "marriage covenant." God joins those who commit to each other to be companions, but if one (or both) decides to divorce (right or wrong) they are divorced.

14. **The idea that a marriage is non-dissolvable may or may not have come from the Roman Catholic Church in all cases, but it most certainly did not come from the Bible. Jesus said "let not" man separate what God has joined. He did not say man "cannot" separate what God has joined.** An unlawful divorce is still a divorce. God does not hold a couple "hostage" when it comes to the marriage covenant. We are marriage partners, not married prisoners. We are mutual companions, not mindless captives.

15. When a couple decides to "be joined together" in marriage, God will "join" them. And when a couple (one or both) decides that they no longer want to be "joined together," then God recognizes that they are no longer joined together. *The very idea that God keeps a couple "joined together" who are no longer "joined together" is absolutely absurd.*

8

WHAT IS INVOLVED IN BEING A COMPANION IN MARRIAGE?

1. So far we have learned that, according to Malachi 2:14, marriage is a "covenant" or agreement (pledge/promise/ vow) to be a "companion" to our mate for life. But what is involved in being a marital companion? I believe that it can be briefly summarized in three categories.

2. Marriage provides a *social companion*. The reason God instituted marriage is because it was not good for man to be alone (Gen. 2:18a). He needed a "companion" who was "comparable" to and suited for him (Gen. 2:18b). He needed a friend. That friend should be our marriage companion. The friend who "loves at all times" should be the companion that we choose and promise to spend our lives with.

3. There is a song by Bill Withers that I have always liked titled, "Lean on Me." The song emphasizes that we all need somebody to lean on. The married woman in the Song of Solomon said this about her husband: "*His mouth is sweetness itself; he is altogether lovely. This is my lover, this is my*

friend, O daughters of Jerusalem" (Song of Solomon 5:16). This is what true companionship involves. It is being friends as well as lovers. Blessed indeed are those who marry their best friend. They will always have a social companion. A marriage partner is indeed somebody to lean on.

4. We need somebody to lean on for joy. A true friend/companion brings joy. Webster's definition of a friend is "one attached to another by affection or esteem." Marriage companions are a joy to have. *"Perfume and incense bring joy to the heart and pleasantness of one's friend springs from his earnest counsel"* (Prov. 27:9). This verse indicates, among other things, that as perfume brings "joy to the heart," so does the "pleasantness of one's friend." Our mates should be our very best and closest friend on earth. Marital companionship provides joy.

5. We need somebody to lean on for support. We all need somebody who supports and encourages us when the "chips are down." We need someone who will help us when times are bad. *"For if they fall, one will lift up his companion. But woe to him who is alone when he falls, for he has no one to help him up."* (Ecc.4:10). This is what true marital companionship is all about. It is about helping each other out.

6. We need somebody to lean on for understanding. We all need somebody who understands. *"A friend loves at all times, and a brother is born for adversity"* (Prov. 17:17). A friend/companion loves at all times because they understand. Someone has said, "A friend is a person who knows all about you, yet loves you anyway." There was a contest to define the word "friend" and the winning definition read: "A friend is

the one who comes in when the whole world has gone out." We all need a marriage companion/friend who understands.

7. We need somebody to lean on who will stay. We all need somebody who will stand by us and stick with us come what may. *"A man who has friends must himself be friendly, but there is a friend who sticks closer than a brother"* (Prov.18:24). One of the true marks of a companion/friend is that they are there when there is every reason for them not to be. As Proverbs 17:17 puts it, *"A friend loves at all times..."* This should surely be true of our marriage partners.

8. Marriage provides a *sexual companion.* It is interesting and exciting that the first (not the fourth, third, or second, but the very "first") recorded command ever given to any man on any subject was given to a husband and his wife and it had to do with the sexual relationship. Read the account for yourself:

> *So God created man in His own image; in the image of God He created him; male and female He created them. Then God blessed them, and God said to them, **"Be fruitful and multiply;** fill the earth..."* (Gen. 1:27-28).

9. The man and his wife were both naked and not ashamed. This is what the marriage relationship is partly about! Read it for yourself:

> *Therefore a man shall leave his father and mother and be joined to his wife, and they shall become one flesh. And they were **both naked,***

the man and his wife, and were not ashamed. (Gen. 2:24-25).

10. It was only with the involvement of sin that sex in marriage was corrupted. It is the same today. Sex in marriage is what real sex is all about. It is God's way of fulfilling the sexual needs of men and women. If there is any shame involved in the sexual relationship in marriage it is, most likely, because one or both of the marriage partners has been influenced by sinful attitudes about sex or uninformed about marital sex. I tell our young people that when God says "flee sexual immorality" (1 Cor. 6:18), He is not trying to keep you "from" sex, but is trying to keep sex "for" you in the marital relationship where it can be experienced and enjoyed without guilt or shame.

11. Marriage is an honorable state and the marriage bed is undefiled. *"Marriage is honorable among all, and the bed undefiled; but fornicators and adulterers God will judge"* (Heb. 13:4).

12. The Song of Solomon is a book about married love. In my survey of the books of the Bible, I title it "A Gift from Above is called Married Love." This book by Solomon more than any other section of the Bible focuses on what married love is all about and emphasizes the importance and prominence of sex in marriage. The book stresses the importance of married couples being friends and lovers (sexual companions) in the following words. *"His mouth is most sweet, yes, he is altogether lovely. This is my beloved, and this is my friend..."* (Song 5:16).

13. Marriage should provide a *spiritual companion*. God's ideal and original plan was and is that husbands and wives be *"heirs together of the grace of life"* (1 Pet. 3:7). Today He wants us to be spiritually united in Christ. Of course, we are still married whether we are spiritual companions or not (1 Pet. 3:1; 1 Cor. 7:12ff), but it is still God's original and ideal plan for men and women.

14. There is much more that could be written about what it takes to make and maintain a good marriage. The Bible has a lot to say on this subject that will help. There are many good books and other teaching materials along this line that are easy to find. But this book is primarily about what the Bible teaches about MDR. Therefore, because of time and space this one chapter is all we will write on this point.

9

WHAT HAPPENS WHEN MAN DEPARTS FROM GOD'S ORIGINAL PLAN?

1. When men departed from God's original plan because of sin, God then began to regulate or impose boundaries around mankind's behavior. The Bible is about God dealing with the problem of sin—bringing His Son in the world to save us all and seeking to get us back on the right track. After sin entered the world, God allowed and regulated many things that were not in harmony with His ideal will or plans. Sin ruined everything in a sense.

2. Man sinned in violating God's ideal will for his good, and this ultimately brought about polygamy, divorce, remarriage, and numerous other marital issues. But God still had man's ultimate good in mind and so He regulated man's conduct so it would work best for him in light of his continuing sinful condition. God began to reveal what might be called His "permissive will" to educate and restrain man from making matters worse. In other words, **He permitted things that**

were not according to His ideal will or His original plan for man. The things that God permitted or allowed were not sinful, but neither were they according to what God intended from the beginning. It is important to understand that everything that God tells us to do is for our own good. God made that clear when He inspired Moses to say:

> *And now, Israel, what does the Lord your God require of you, but to fear the Lord your God, to walk in all His ways and to love Him, to serve the Lord your God with all your heart and with all your soul, and to keep the commandments of the Lord and His statutes which I command you today **for your good*** (Deut. 10:12-13).

3. God had regulations for MDR in both the Old Testament and the New but we must keep it mind that it is always for our own good and what is best in light of man's sinful nature.

10

Is Divorcing a Mate Always Wrong?

1. An "unauthorized" divorce is wrong. In other words, divorcing without God's sanction and/or approval is sinful and wrong. All lawlessness is sin. If a person violates or transgresses God's law on any matter—marriage or otherwise—it is wrong. *"Whoever commits sin also commits lawlessness, and sin is lawlessness"* (1 John 3:4).

2. But the fact is that God Himself has authorized (given the right to) some to divorce their mates. Divorce is an option in some cases. The following are some examples.

3. In the case where a mate is married to a "sexually immoral" person, Jesus said an innocent party can divorce them. Surely it would not be wrong to do something that Jesus gave one the right to do. I know, of course, that in most cases it would be better to "forgive and forget," if the sexually immoral person repented, but keeping the marriage intact is not "required" in those cases and it is not possible in all cases. But that is beside the point in this discussion. The main point here is

that Jesus does indeed "authorize" those who are married to fornicators or those guilty of sexual immorality to divorce their mates. See Matthew 19:9.

4. The Holy Spirit also authorizes a deserted believer to divorce a mate who has abandoned the marriage covenant. In 1 Corinthians 7:15, Paul plainly said that the believer is "not under bondage" to an unbeliever who "departs." Surely this means that the believer is allowed to divorce a mate who has abandoned the marriage covenant. Since God said that the believer is no longer bound to the unbeliever, it could not be wrong for the believer to "make it legal and official" if need be through divorce. *"But to the rest I, not the Lord, say: If any brother has a wife who does not believe, and she is willing to live with him, let him not divorce her"* (1 Cor. 7:12). Note that, even though the Lord did not specifically deal with this situation when He was on earth, the inspired apostle said that if the unbelieving wife "is willing to live with" her believing husband," he is not to "divorce her." But the obvious implication is that if she is not "willing to live with him," then he can, with God's sanction/approval, "divorce" her. Read what is being said and do not allow past or present misunderstandings to cloud the issue. "If she is willing to live with him" let him not "divorce" her. But if she is *not* willing to live with him in the marriage relationship, then he can "divorce" her. How much simpler could that be?

5. Furthermore, God commanded His people to divorce their marriage partners who had led them astray in the Old Testament. He has never demanded or even allowed His people to stay in any relationship (marriage or otherwise) that caused them to sin against or turn away from Him.

6. The reason that God did not allow the Israelites to marry the Canaanites is because they would turn the hearts of the children of Israel away from Him.

> *Nor shall you make marriages with them. You shall not give your daughter to their son, nor take their daughter for your son.* **For they will turn your sons away from following Me**, *to serve other gods; so the anger of the Lord will be aroused against you and destroy you suddenly.* (Deut. 7:3-4).

7. Observe that the main reason they were not to "make marriages" was "for" a certain reason. What was the reason? *"For they will turn your sons away from following me, to serve other gods."* It was not wrong to marry a Canaanite if the Canaanite became a believer in God. Rahab (one of the worst in Canaan) became a believer (Heb. 11:31; Jas. 2:25) and married an Israelite named Salmon. Jesus was born in that lineage (Matt. 1:5). The reason it was wrong to marry them was because they would lead them away from God. It was not necessarily the "marriage" that was wrong, but what the marriages would do in most cases.

8. Later, Ruth (a Moabite) became a believer (Ruth 1:16) and she married Boaz (an Israelite). Again, Jesus was born in that lineage (Matt. 1:5). So the reason for forbidding marriage was not simply who they were by *race*, but what they would do in *religion*.

9. However, when the children of Israel did marry those who caused them to sin and turn away from God, they were told to "divorce" their wives—even if they had children by them.

*When these things were done, the leaders came to me, saying, "The people of Israel and the priests and the Levites have not separated themselves from the peoples of the lands, **with respect to the abominations of the Canaanites**, the Hittites, the Perizzites, the Jebusites, the Ammonites, the Moabites, the Egyptians, and the Amorites. For they have taken some of their daughters as wives for themselves and their sons, so that the holy seed is mixed with the peoples of those lands. Indeed, the hand of the leaders and rulers has been foremost in this trespass."* (Ezra 9:1-2).

10. Observe that these marriages were not like the marriages to Rahab or Ruth. Rather, these marriages resulted in the Israelites turning away from God by being involved in the "abominations of the Canaanites."

11. So, what did God require them to do in this situation?

*Now while Ezra was praying, and while he was confessing, weeping, and bowing down before the house of God, a very large assembly of men, women, and children gathered to him from Israel; for the people wept very bitterly. And Shechaniah the son of Jehiel, one of the sons of Elam, spoke up and said to Ezra, "We have trespassed against our God, and have taken pagan wives from the peoples of the land; yet now there is hope in Israel in spite of this. 3 Now therefore, **let us make a covenant with***

*our God to put away all these wives and those
who have been born to them, according to the
advice of my master and of those who tremble
at the commandment of our God; and let it be
done according to the law*. (Ezra 10:1-3).

12. They were commanded by Ezra, the priest of God, to divorce those "pagan wives." Observe the reading:

*Then Ezra the priest stood up and said to them,
"You have transgressed and have taken pagan
wives, adding to the guilt of Israel. 11 Now
therefore, make confession to the Lord God of
your fathers, and do His will; separate yourselves from the peoples of the land, and from
the pagan wives."* (Ezra 10:10-11).

13. Here again we see that all divorce is not sinful. Some divorces are authorized and commanded by God as was the case here during Ezra's time. The same thing happened later on with the Jews when Nehemiah came to Jerusalem. They had "married women of Ashdod, Ammon, and Moab."

*In those days I also saw Jews who had married
women of Ashdod, Ammon, and Moab. And half
of their children spoke the language of Ashdod,
and could not speak the language of Judah, but
spoke according to the language of one or the
other people. So I contended with them and
cursed them, struck some of them and pulled
out their hair, and made them swear by God,
saying, "You shall not give your daughters as*

*wives to their sons, nor take their daughters for your sons or yourselves. Did not Solomon king of Israel sin by these things? Yet among many nations there was no king like him, who was beloved of his God; and God made him king over all Israel. Nevertheless **pagan women caused even him to sin**. Should we then hear of your doing all this great evil, **transgressing against our God by marrying pagan women**?"* (Neh. 13:23-27).

14. The clear indication in these verses is that just as Solomon's wives "caused even him to sin," so these wives had done the same thing to the Jews and they were *"doing all this great evil, transgressing against our God by marrying pagan women."*

15. What did Nehemiah do to correct this? He *"cleansed them of everything pagan"* (Neh. 13:30). This surely suggests that they did the same thing that the Jews did in Ezra's time, and that was separate (divorce) themselves "from the pagan wives" (Ezra 10:10-11). Therefore, this obviously is another case of "divorce" with God's sanction and approval.

16. We also need to realize that the prophet Malachi was most likely a contemporary with Nehemiah and was condemning the same thing that Nehemiah was. Observe that he condemns this very sin:

Have we not all one Father? Has not one God created us? Why do we deal treacherously with one another by profaning the covenant of the *fathers? Judah has dealt treacherously, and an abomination has been committed in Israel and in Jerusalem, For Judah has profaned The Lord's holy institution which He loves: He has **married the daughter of a foreign god**.* (Malachi 2:10-11)

17. Malachi condemned them for marrying the "daughter" (worshipper/one in a relationship) with a foreign god. This is the very thing that God has never allowed. He has never allowed His children to remain in any marriage (or other relationship) that resulted in His children turning away from Him.

18. Another interesting point in this discussion that is worth mentioning here is the fact that Malachi condemns the Jews who had "treacherously" put away their Jewish wives in this very instance in order to marry these "pagan wives" who were causing them to sin.

*And this is the second thing you do: You cover the altar of the Lord with tears, with weeping and crying; so He does not regard the offering anymore, nor receive it with goodwill from your hands. Yet you say, "For what reason?" Because the Lord has been witness between you and the wife of your youth, with whom you have **dealt treacherously**; yet she is your companion and your wife by covenant. But did He not make them one, having a remnant of the Spirit? And why one? He seeks godly offspring. Therefore take heed to your spirit, and let none **deal treacherously** with the wife of his youth.*

> *"For the Lord God of Israel says That He hates divorce, For it covers one's garment with violence," says the Lord of hosts. "Therefore take heed to your spirit, that you do not **deal treacherously**."* (Mal. 2:13-16).

19. Observe, that according to Malachi, God hates and condemns "divorce" when they were "treacherously" divorcing their faithful Jewish wives in order to marry these pagan wives. But He commanded and approved of these same Jews separating from (divorcing) their pagan wives who had caused them to sin against Him, according to both Ezra and Nehemiah.

20. It is also important to note that God has not changed at all in this matter. **He still sanctions and approves of divorcing a mate if that mate is causing His children to sin and turn away from Him.** For example, notice again what Paul said concerning a believer being married to an unbeliever in 1 Corinthians 7:12-13:

> *But to the rest I, not the Lord, say: If any brother has a wife who does not believe, and she is willing to live with him, let him not divorce her. And a woman who has a husband, who does not believe, **if he is willing to live with** her, let her **not divorce** him.*

21. The command is clear that if the unbeliever is "willing to live" with a faithful believer, then the believer is not to "divorce" the unbeliever. But what if the unbeliever is not willing and is causing the believer to sin by staying with him/

her? What happens then? The believer can, in those cases, "divorce" the unbeliever rather than being led away from God.

22. Suppose, for example, that a Christian wife is married to an unbeliever who converts to a pagan religion and he demands that she and their children be brought up in that religion. Must she stay in that marriage, be involved in that religion and allow her children to be taught and reared in that? I think not! Can she divorce him with God's approval? I believe she can and should, if the relationship is causing her to turn away from God! The same would be true in any relationship (marriage or otherwise) and it would not matter what the issue is — whether being involved in a false religion or insisting that she sin in other ways. We cannot love father, mother, children or wife/husband more than God (Mt. 10:34-37; Lk. 14:26).

23. The thing we must remember is that God does not demand or desire that His children remain in any relationship that leads them away from Him. As a matter of fact, He said exactly that in 2 Corinthians 6:14-17:

> *Do not be **unequally yoked** together with unbe-lievers. For what fellowship has righteous-ness with lawlessness? And what communion has light with darkness? And what accord has Christ with Belial? Or what part has a believer with an unbeliever? And what agreement has the temple of God with idols? For you are the temple of the living God. As God has said: "I will dwell in them and walk among them. I will be their God, and they shall be my people."*

> *Therefore "**Come out from** among them and be separate, says the Lord. Do not touch what is unclean, and I will receive you."*

24. Any "yoke" that causes us to have "fellowship" (participate) in lawlessness and have "communion" (share) with darkness, and puts us in "accord" (agreement) with Satan must be severed. We must "come out from" any relationship (idolatry, marriage, or otherwise) that causes us to sin against and turn away from God.

25. Someone may object and say 2 Corinthians 6:14-17 does not apply to marriage but to idolatry. The primary reference is to idolatry without question—but it is not limited to idolatry. A Christian cannot remain in *any yoke* that causes them to sin. Furthermore, what if an unbelieving spouse gets involved in idolatry and demands that the believer be involved? Could the believer divorce them then? The command is clear: *"Come out from among them."*

11

ARE THOSE IN AN UNAUTHORIZED DIVORCE "STILL MARRIED" IN GOD'S SIGHT?

1. It is obvious that God authorizes divorce in certain circumstances or for certain reasons as we have already learned. But He does not authorize divorce for just "any and every cause." He does not allow or sanction the putting away of a faithful mate unless there is a scriptural reason. But what if a person divorces a mate on grounds other than "sexual immorality" or "desertion" etc. is that couple "still married" to each other as far as God is concerned? **If so, since when is doing something God said not to do, not really done?**

2. The idea that the one who is "divorced" is not really "put away," but is "still married" to the one who put them away makes absolutely no sense at all. Jesus did not say man "cannot" separate what God has joined, but He said "let not" man separate (Mt. 19:6). I know that some say they are "still married" in "God's sight" but the fact is God is not blind! An unauthorized divorce is still a divorce! And unless the blind

lead the blind into thinking that God is blind, we all ought to be able to "see" it. Since when can we actually do something that God says not to do in God's sight (plain view) and it is not really done because He does not approve of it?

3. If they are "still married" in God's sight, what is wrong with divorcing? If God does not see it, or recognize it, or admit that it has happened, then why is it wrong? According to this view, Jesus said, "What therefore God has joined together, let not man divorce, but even if you do divorce it means nothing, because you are 'still married' in God's sight." That would be like saying, "Whom God has given life, let not man murder; but even if you do murder it means nothing, because they are "still alive" in God's sight."

4. Is God ignorant of what is going on? If someone is murdered, they are not still alive in anybody's sight—especially God's. This is why it is sinful to murder. If someone is divorced, they are not still married in anybody's sight—especially God's. This is why it is wrong to divorce in these cases. It is a false and silly idea to say that when two people get a divorce for a reason other than "fornication" or "desertion" etc. they are "still married" in God's sight. The truth is they are not married in anybody's sight that can see things as they are.

5. In 1 Corinthians 7:10-11, God told those who are married not to divorce, but if they did, they were to "remain unmarried." In verse 10 He said, "Do not divorce." But in verse 11 He saw (He was not blind to reality) that if they were to divorce then they would be "unmarried" because

they divorced. When someone does something God said not to do, it is still actually done!

6. Do we actually believe that God goes blind? Why do I ask that? It is because of the ridiculous idea that when two people get a divorce for a reason other than "fornication," they are "still married" in God's sight. The truth is they are not married in anybody's sight that can see things as they are. **God is not blind to the sins and decisions that man makes even when He disapproves of those choices and decisions.**

7. Christians are those who have "joined" themselves to the Lord (Zech. 2:11; 1 Cor. 6:17). Therefore, as part of the church, they are "one flesh" with the Lord (Eph. 5:31-32). But they can have an "evil heart of unbelief in departing from God" (Heb. 3:12), and they will no longer be "joined" to or "one flesh" with the Lord. There is no "invisible clamp" or "unwritten law" or "mystical magnet" that will keep them "joined together" with Christ against their wills. The same is true with those whom God has "joined together" in marriage.

8. Just because a divorce is unauthorized does not mean that it is unreal. And just because God does not allow it to happen with His approval, does not mean that He does not acknowledge that it did happen in spite of His disapproval. *Since when is doing something God said not to do, not really done?*

12

WHAT IS THE MEANING OF THE WORD "ADULTERY" IN THE BIBLE?

1. This is one of the most important questions to answer when it comes to the MDR discussion. A lot hinges on this word. What does it mean and how is it used?

2. Adultery is a "covenant" word as used in the Bible and not just a sexual word. It has a much broader meaning than just having sex. It can and does refer to sex but, even then, there is a covenant involved. For example, if two young unmarried people have sex, the Bible does not refer to that as "adultery," but as "fornication." When the word "adultery" is used it is because one or both of the parties are in a "covenant" (or marriage relationship) with someone else.

3. What is the definition of the word "adultery"? The dictionary says it is "a sexual encounter or relationship between a married person and someone other than their spouse" (http://www.merriam-webster.com/thesaurus/adultery). The word

is used numerous times in the Bible to refer to a "sexual encounter" between a "married person and someone other than their spouse" but that is not always the case. Like many other words, "adultery" is sometimes used "metaphorically." A metaphor is "a word for one thing that is used to refer to another thing in order to show or suggest that they are similar." One example among many is the word "leaven." The primary meaning is "a substance that makes dough rise." But Jesus used it metaphorically to refer to the "teaching" of the Scribes and Pharisees (Mt. 16:12). Paul used it metaphorically to refer to sinful influences in the church (1 Cor. 5:6-7). Therefore it does not always refer to "a substance that makes dough rise." It is used in other ways.

4. **Words mean what the Bible interprets them to mean regardless of what the present day dictionaries and lexicons might say.** An example of this point is the word "hate." Look up the definition of the word "hate" in the dictionary or Bible concordance and apply the meaning it gives to Luke 14:26 where God says to "hate" your father and mother. Jesus did not use the word "hate" in its usual sense according to the dictionaries. Then see the definition the Bible gives in Matthew 10:37 of "love less" and you can see what Jesus actually means.

5. In the same way, the word "adultery" does not always mean what a dictionary or concordance may say it means. It will say adultery is a "sexual encounter" with "someone other than a spouse." But it does not always mean that in the Bible. In the Bible it can refer to "thoughts" and "desires" about having sex with another. Jesus said, *"But I say to you*

that whoever looks at a woman to lust for her has already **committed adultery** *with her* **in his heart**" (Mt. 5:28).

6. Here "adultery" is committed "in the heart" and not literally by a "sexual encounter" with "someone else." Here the word for one thing –"a sexual encounter between a married person and someone other than their spouse"—is used for another thing which is "sexual desires" involving only one person and is similar to (but not exactly like) a sexual encounter with someone else. This is how a word is used "metaphorically."

7. Furthermore, the word "adultery" is not always used in the Bible to refer to "sex" at all. Sometimes it is neither physical nor mental sexual activity. Many times the word is used to refer to faithlessness or spiritually breaking a covenant with God which is metaphorically called "adultery."

8. Read carefully the following verse: *"So it came to pass, through her casual harlotry, that she defiled the land and* **committed adultery** *with* **stones and trees**" (Jer. 3:9). Note that this verse clearly says that Israel "committed adultery" with "stones and trees." There is nothing "sexual" about this. They were not having sex with stones or trees. They had broken their covenant with God to worship idols and it is called "adultery." Here again the word for one thing—"a sexual encounter between a married person and someone other than their spouse"—is used for another thing, which is breaking a covenant with God to worship idols. It is similar to (but not exactly like) a sexual encounter with someone else in that it involves breaking a covenant in order to do it. The word "adultery" is used "metaphorically" to refer to the

"spiritual adultery" they had committed. But it had nothing to do with sex.

9. In Ezekiel 6:9 we read the following indictment of God against Israel:

> *I was crushed by their **adulterous heart** which has departed from me, and by their eyes which play the harlot after their idols; they will loathe themselves for the evils which they committed in all their abominations.*

10. Their adulterous heart in this passage had nothing to do with sex. It was by lusting after "their idols" by which they departed from God, and that is referred to as "adultery." Why? Because it involved faithlessness to the covenant that they had made with God.

11. God "entered a covenant" (Ezek. 16:8) with Jerusalem, but Jerusalem became "an adulterous wife" (Ezek. 16:32). Therefore, God judged her "as women who break wedlock" (Ezek. 16:38) because they had "despised the oath by breaking the covenant" (Ezek. 16:59). Why were they adulterous? It was not because of the physical act of sex. It was because they had broken the covenant they had made with God and were going after idols. **"Adultery" always includes a violation of a covenant in some way.**

12. Ezekiel 23:37 reads as follows:

> *For they have **committed adultery**, and blood is on their hands. They have committed adultery*

*with their idols, and even **sacrificed their sons**
whom they bore to Me, passing them through
the fire, to devour them.*

13. How had they "committed adultery"? Was it by having "a sexual encounter with someone other than a spouse"? No! It was by having their children sacrificed to idols. Killing children in a fire has nothing to do with sex. Yet it is called "adultery." Why? Because it involved faithlessness toward God and violating the covenant they had with Him.

14. In the New Testament, James used the words "adulterers" and "adulteresses" to refer to violating a covenant with God for friendship with the world. James wrote:

> ***Adulterers** and **adulteresses**! Do you not know
> that friendship with the world is enmity with
> God? Whoever therefore wants to be a **friend
> of the world** makes himself an enemy of God*
> (Jam. 4:4).

15. Observe carefully that they are called "adulterers" and "adulteresses" because of their "friendship with the world" and not because they were having sex with someone other than their spouse. Strong's Concordance says that the word "adulterers" is used here metaphorically for "one who is faithless toward God."

16. When we understand that "adultery" is used to refer to faithlessness to a covenant or a violation of a covenant, then we can see how the word is used in the Bible and especially as it relates to MDR. *The word "adultery" always involves*

covenant breaking or faithlessness, but it does not always involve sex. Notice how the word is used in the Bible.

17. First, there is *physical adultery*. This adultery involves covenant breaking or faithlessness by having a sexual encounter with someone other than a spouse. The religious leaders caught a woman in the act of physical adultery.

> *Then the scribes and Pharisees brought to Him a woman caught in adultery. And when they had set her in the midst, they said to Him, "Teacher, this woman was caught in **adultery**, in the very **act*** (Jn. 8:3-4).

> *"The man who **commits adultery with** another man's wife, he who commits adultery with his neighbor's wife, the adulterer and the adulteress, shall surely be put to death* (Lev. 20:10).

> *Whoever **commits adultery with** a woman lacks understanding; he who does so destroys his own soul* (Prov. 6:32).

All of these references to "committing adultery" involve breaking a marriage covenant by engaging in the physical act of sex with someone other than a spouse.

18. Second, there is *mental adultery*. This adultery involves covenant breaking by lusting for sex in the heart, but does not refer to committing the physical act of sex with someone else.

> *"You have heard that it was said to those of old, 'You shall not commit adultery.' But I say to you that whoever **looks at a woman to lust** for her has already **committed adultery** with her in his heart.* (Mt. 5:27-28).

> *Do not lust after her beauty **in your heart**, nor let her allure you with her eyelids. For by means of a harlot a man is reduced to a crust of bread; and an **adulteress** will prey upon his precious life.* (Prov. 6:25-26).

These references to "committing adultery" involve mentally breaking a marriage covenant by lusting after another man's wife or by a married man lusting after a woman other than his wife.

19. Third, there is *spiritual adultery.* This adultery involves covenant breaking or faithlessness to God, but does not involve sex at all.

> *So it came to pass, through her casual harlotry, that she defiled the land and **committed adultery** with **stones and trees**.* (Jeremiah 3:9).

> *For they have **committed adultery,** and blood is on their hands. They have committed adultery with their idols, and even **sacrificed their sons** whom they bore to me, passing them through the fire, to devour them.* (Ezekiel. 23:37).

__Adulterers__ and __adulteresses__! Do you not know that friendship with the world is enmity with God? Whoever therefore wants to be a __friend of the world__ makes himself an enemy of God (James 4:4).

These references to "committing adultery" involve spiritually breaking a covenant with God and do not involve sex at all. Spiritual adultery is still "adultery" because it involves faithlessness to a covenant or a violation of a covenant.

20. Fourth, there is *marital adultery*. This adultery involves covenant breaking or faithlessness to the marriage covenant, but not necessarily to the sex act.

And I say to you, whoever __divorces__ his wife, except for sexual immorality, and marries another, __commits adultery__; and whoever marries her who is divorced commits adultery." (Matt. 19:9).

So He said to them, "Whoever __divorces__ his wife and marries another commits adultery __against her__ (Mark 10:11).

These references to "committing adultery" involve breaking a marital covenant with a mate in order to marry someone else. Marital adultery is still "adultery" because it involves faithlessness to a covenant or a violation of a covenant with a marriage companion. But it does not always involve sex! For example, a man who is too old for sex, if he divorces his faithful wife and marries someone else, he "commits

73

adultery" against his wife because he has broken the marital covenant with her in order to marry someone else—even if he never has sex with his new wife.

13

What About Marriage and Divorce Under the Law of Moses?

1. It is important to keep in mind that marriage is a "covenant relationship" between a man and a woman. That is, the two agree to be companions for life. God's original plan has never changed. His ideal will is one man for one woman as companions for life in every dispensation of time.

2. However, because of man's sinfulness, God must regulate man's conduct for man's own good, which allows for numerous things that are less than ideal but not sinful.

3. **One of the first things we learn about marriage from the Law of Moses is that marriage is not a license to mistreat and abuse a marriage partner.** We are partners, not prisoners. We are companions, not captives. Even slaves who married their owners were not to be abused or mistreated in the marriage relationship. This is one of the first things

that Moses taught concerning marriage immediately after recording the Ten Commandments:

> *If he takes another wife, he shall **not diminish** her food, her **clothing**, and her **marriage rights**. And if he does not do these three for her, then she shall go out free, without paying money* (Ex. 21:10-11).

4. Observe that the husband was not to diminish or withhold or deprive (NIV) his wife (even if he took another wife) of three things. He could not starve her or fail to provide clothing (necessities of life) for her or deny her "marriage rights." Marriage rights would include sexual companionship. If he failed to provide these three things she could go out free without paying money to be free.

5. The point is that she could "go out" and would not be bound to him if he deprived her of these three things. We must understand that God did not require one to stay in a marriage where they are abused, neglected, or refused marriage rights. Two reasons for marriage is social and sexual companionship. Thus God did not require a wife to stay in a relationship with a husband who deprived her of these things. I also realize that this point can be abused and misused. There are no perfect marriage partners and no partner should get everything they want at all times, but neither should there be total neglect or abuse in these matters. Some might use this to mistreat or divorce a mate because they do not conform to their every wish and want and that would be an abuse and misuse of the passage. But the fact that some may have

abused the regulation in Moses' day did not keep Moses from teaching it and it should not keep us from teaching it today.

6. Just because a person is married does not mean that they must put up with abuse. The idea of having to stay with a mate no matter how they treat you is not taught in the Old Testament or the New. We understand that marriage is *for* life—but not if it *endangers your life*. Surely God does not expect us to remain in wedlock with a mate who keeps us in a headlock. I know that some fathers and mothers would say, "If he beats my daughter, I will kill him." But the obvious implication from this statement is that God would rather us kill him than for her to divorce him, which is surely not true.

7. Marriage was designed for mutual habitation, not for brutal intimidation. **For one to teach that God demands a wife/ husband to remain in an abusive marriage relationship is itself abusive.** It is an indisputable fact that marriage is not an indissoluble act and never has been. Moses did not say it and Jesus did not teach it. Sometimes the only sensible and scriptural recourse is a quick and permanent divorce from an abusive partner.

8. We are mutual companions, but not mindless captives. If we want our mate to stay with us, we need to act like it!

9. Moses did later regulate divorce because of the "hardness" of the hearts of those married and their sinful desire to put away their mates. In doing so, he only allowed the Jews to put away mates who were guilty of some "uncleanness." They had to give her a "bill of divorcement" which would allow her to marry someone else and they could not

take her back after she was married to someone else. In that culture, this last restriction most likely would cause them to think twice before putting their wives away in order to marry someone else. (See Deut. 24:1-4).

10. Some object to the "uncleanness" referring to "fornication" or physical adultery because the penalty for that sin was death (Lev. 20:10; Deut. 22:22). But the death penalty was only enforceable in very rare cases. The death penalty for any sin worthy of death had to be on the testimony of "two or three witnesses" and never on the testimony of "one witness" (Deut. 17:6-7). The witnesses had to be first to throw the stones at her (Jn. 8:7). Therefore, if the husband was the only "witness" then all he could do was put her away for her uncleanness. Furthermore, Jesus Himself said that it referred to "sexual immorality" and that should settle the matter (Matt. 19:1-9).

14

Did Jesus Change What Moses Taught Regarding God's Moral Law for Man?

1. The answer to the above question is: absolutely not! In fact, when Jesus first began teaching, He warned against changing anything that Moses taught along these lines.

> **Do not think that I came to destroy the Law** or the Prophets. I did not come to destroy but to fulfill. For assuredly, I say to you, till heaven and earth pass away, one jot or one tittle will by no means pass from the law till all is fulfilled. **Whoever** therefore **breaks one of the least of these commandments**, and **teaches men so**, shall be called least in the kingdom of heaven; but whoever does and teaches them, he shall be called great in the kingdom of heaven. (Matt. 5:18-19).

2. In these verses, Jesus condemns those who would "break one" of the commandments given through Moses as well as the one who "teaches men" to break them while He was on earth. Surely, then, He did not break them Himself and He certainly did not teach other men to break them. Did He? If He did, He was self-condemned in His own sermon and by His own words!! But we know that is not true and therefore all that He taught in the "Sermon on the Mount" was for the purpose of showing them what God *meant* when He spoke through Moses.

3. Furthermore, when He was concluding the teaching He did in Matthew chapters 5-7, He said it could be summed up in one verse: *"Therefore, whatever you want men to do to you, do also to them, for **this is the Law and the Prophets"*** (Matt. 7:12).

4. The word "Therefore" carries us back to what He had been teaching throughout the sermon. *The "golden rule" sums up what God has always expected of man*—which is what Moses and Jesus both taught. It is not only what the "Law and the Prophets" taught in the realm of morality, but also what Jesus reaffirmed in His teaching. Loving your neighbor as yourself is the "royal law" taught both by Moses and by Jesus (James 2:8; Mt. 22:36-40).

5. We must understand that, in the Sermon on the Mount, when Jesus said things like, *"you have heard that it was said by those of old"* (Matt. 5:21, 27, 31, etc.), **He was not talking about what "Moses" said and taught, but what the "Scribes and Pharisees" were saying and teaching and had been teaching for years.** As the religious teachers

of the day, they had misunderstood, misapplied, and mis-used most of the things that God had intended in the moral requirements of the Law of Moses. They had either changed God's moral commands altogether or misapplied what God had said in the commands. This is what Jesus was correcting in His teaching.

6. The Law of Moses was "holy and just and good" in its moral precepts and commandments (Rom. 7:12). God did not create sin by giving the law through Moses. Sin already existed long before the Law of Moses was given. The Law *revealed* sin, but it did not *create* sin (Rom. 3:20). The Law defined what sin is (Rom. 7:7) and therefore showed man how many ways he did sin and how bad he actually is (Rom. 7:19).

7. In other words, *it has always been wrong* to murder, steal, bear false witness, covet a neighbor's wife, commit adul-tery, etc. These things were wrong from the very beginning of time. It was not right for Cain to murder his brother (Gen. 4:8; 1 Jn. 3:12). It was not right for Abraham to lie or bear false witness about his wife (Gen. 12:12-13). It was not right for Pharaoh to commit adultery with Abraham's wife (Gen. 12:18) or for Abimelech to have Isaac's wife (Gen. 26:9-10). It was not right for Jacob to fail to honor his father (Gen. 27). These sins were all being committed long before the Law of Moses was given. And they are still being committed today and are just as wrong now as they have ever been.

8. Jesus reaffirmed and kept all of the Ten Commandments and did not change any of them "until they were all (not some, many, or most, but ALL) fulfilled by His death on

the cross. He did not break them or teach others to break them when He was on earth. He kept them perfectly and taught others to do the same. **He also reaffirmed nine of them as part of His teaching in the New Testament**. The only exception was keeping the Sabbath. This one command related only to the Jewish nation and their deliverance from Egyptian bondage (Deut. 5:12-15; Ex. 31:16-17) and was a type of our rest in Christ and ultimately our rest in Heaven (Heb. 4:3-10).

9. The other nine commandments are repeated verbatim in the New Testament (Rom. 13:8-10; Eph. 6:2). Why? Because they involve the principles of right and wrong which have existed from the beginning of time. Moses taught them and Jesus reaffirmed them. Note: Jesus did not reaffirm as part of the New Testament everything that Moses taught in the Old Testament (such as, animal sacrifices, polygamy, death by stoning, etc.) but He did reaffirm the moral principles involved in the Ten Commandments...including marriage, divorce and remarriage. (Matt. 19:1-9).

Note: For more on this subject see Appendix number three: WHAT IS JESUS CORRECTING IN THE SERMON ON THE MOUNT?

15

WHAT ABOUT THE PHARISEES AND THEIR TEACHING ABOUT DIVORCE AND REMARRIAGE?

1. The Pharisees were saying numerous things that God never said or meant. This is the teaching that Jesus was opposing in the Sermon on the Mount. The Scribes and Pharisees were "hypocrites" (Mt. 23:15) and "blind guides" (Mt. 23:16). They were "evil and adulterous" leaders (Mt. 16:4). They taught as doctrines the "commandments of men" (Mt. 15:8), thus making "of no effect" the commandments of God (Mt. 15:6). They sought to "justify themselves" before men (Lk. 16:15). They were "lovers of money" (Lk. 16:14). They were rotten to the bone inwardly and full of sexual "uncleanness" (Mt. 23:27). Jesus corrected their misguided message and exposed their teaching for what it was.

2. As we study what the Pharisees taught about MDR, it is important to keep in mind that the Pharisees were practicing, teaching or implying the following:

It is not wrong to be angry as long as you do not actually murder someone (Mt. 5:21-26).

It is not wrong to lust in your heart for women or other men's wives (Mt. 5:27-28).

It is not wrong to put away a faithful mate in order to marry someone as long as you give her a certificate of divorce (Mt. 5:31-32).

It is not wrong to swear falsely as long as you swear in the right way (Mt. 5:33-37).

It is not wrong to take personal vengeance against someone who hurts you (Mt. 5:38-42).

It is not wrong to hate your enemies (Mt. 5:43-44).

3. It is no wonder that when Jesus finished the sermon, Matthew records these words:

*And so it was, when Jesus had ended these sayings, that the people were astonished at His teaching, for He taught them as one having authority, and **not as the scribes**.* (Mt. 7:28-29).

4. Jesus had the authority to teach exactly what God had taught all along in the Law of Moses on these moral issues. He did not teach as the scribes and Pharisees had taught when they made of no effect the commandments of God by their traditions and ungodly teaching (Mt. 15:1-14).

5. The Pharisees obviously taught that one could divorce his wife for "just any reason" and therefore violate the covenant with her without sinning in doing so (Mt. 19:3). This is exactly what they had done on numerous other subjects such as swearing, honoring father and mother, personal vengeance, lust, hating enemies, etc. They found a way to change what God had said and that is what they taught others. They taught that there is nothing wrong with divorcing a mate to marry someone else. As long as you give her a "bill of divorcement" you can send her away for just "any" and every cause. Jesus explained that this is exactly the reason Moses gave the commandment about divorce in the first place. It was because of the "hardness of the hearts" of men in dealing with their wives. In Moses' day, they were obviously doing just like the Pharisees were doing in Jesus' day and divorcing their wives for just "any cause." Moses commanded them to give her a "bill of divorcement" and "send her away" if (and only "if") they found some "uncleanness" in her. Observe the reading:

> *When a man takes a wife and marries her, and it happens that she finds no favor in his eyes **because he has found some uncleanness** in her, and he writes her a certificate of divorce, puts it in her hand, and sends her out of his house,* (Deut. 24:1).

6. As in the other cases in the Sermon on the Mount, Jesus did not change the Law of Moses or teach men to violate it on this matter of divorce (Mt. 5:19), Rather, He upheld what Moses taught as being the right thing to do. He said exactly what Moses said. The only reason for divorcing a mate in

order to marry someone else without "committing adultery" against her was if she had been guilty of "sexual immorality" or "uncleanness" herself. Read what He said:

> *They said to Him, "Why then did Moses com-mand to give a certificate of divorce, and to put her away?" He said to them, "Moses, because of the hardness of your hearts, permitted you to divorce your wives, but from the beginning it was not so. And I say to you, whoever divorces his wife, **except for sexual immorality**, and marries another, commits adultery; and who-ever marries her who is divorced commits adul-tery."* (Matt. 19:7-9).

7. Observe that Jesus taught the same thing that Moses taught, but not the same thing that the Pharisees taught. Moses said if a man finds some sexual "uncleanness" in her, he can give her a "certificate of divorce" and send her away. This is exactly what Jesus was saying. She must be guilty of "sexual immorality" in order for you to put her away to marry someone else or else you sin (commit adultery) against her (Mk. 10:11).

8. It is extremely important to understand that Jesus did not teach anything different from Moses concerning the "moral" laws of God. As a matter of fact, the Law of Moses was the "Law of God" and He has never changed His moral law for man because of its intrinsic nature. The Book of Nehemiah makes it perfectly clear that the "Law of Moses" and the "Law of God" is the same Law.

> *Now all the people gathered together as one*
> *man in the open square that was in front of the*
> *Water Gate; and they told Ezra the scribe to*
> *bring the Book of the* **Law of Moses**, *which the*
> *Lord had commanded Israel…So they read dis-*
> *tinctly from the book, in the* **Law of God**; *and*
> *they gave the sense, and helped them to under-*
> *stand the reading.* (Neh. 8:1 & 18).

9. Nine of the Ten Commandments are repeated verbatim in the teaching of the New Testament (Rom. 13:8-10; Eph. 6:2). Why? Because they have always been God's will for man and always will be God's will for man. When James, in the New Testament, said, "*Do not commit adultery*" (James 2:11), he was quoting what God had always said in the Law of Moses which had been true since the beginning of time.

10. The teaching of the Pharisees was not what Moses taught in the law. The Pharisees left out the sexual "uncleanness" of Moses teaching (Deut. 24:1) which Jesus defined as "sexual immorality" (Mt. 19:9).

11. Note carefully what the Pharisees taught and how they left out the "uncleanness" or "sexual immorality" when teaching on the subject: In Matthew 5:31 Jesus, in the Sermon on the Mount, said: "*Furthermore it has been said, 'Whoever divorces his wife, let him give her a certificate of divorce.'*" Jesus said, "It has been said." But who "said" it? It was not Moses. Moses said give her a "bill of divorcement" because you find "some uncleanness in her" (Deut. 24:1). But the Pharisees are the ones who changed that and said that all you have to do is "give her a certificate of divorce" and it does

not matter whether she has done anything wrong or not. As long as you give her a "certificate of divorce" you do not sin or commit adultery against her no matter why you decide to divorce her. She does not have to do anything sexually wrong. She doesn't have to be guilty of "uncleanness" or "sexually immorality." If you give her the bill, then you can divorce her at will.

12. This was the teaching of the Pharisees every time they said anything about it. They always left out the "because he finds some uncleanness in her" part. Read the following verses and see what I mean.

> *Furthermore it has been said* (by the Pharisees), *'Whoever divorces his wife; let him give her a certificate of divorce.'* (Matt. 5:31)

> *They* (Pharisees) *said to Him, "Why then did Moses command to give a certificate of divorce, and to put her away?"* (Matt. 19:7).

> *They* (Pharisees) *said, "Moses permitted a man to write a certificate of divorce, and to dismiss her.* (Mk. 10:4)

13. Observe that they never mentioned her "uncleanness" in any of these references. The teaching of the Pharisees, that one could divorce his wife for just "any cause" without sinning or committing adultery against her, had become so prevalent that the disciples believed that if "any cause" divorce was not true, then it would be best not to marry at all. In other words, if I cannot just put her away "at will"

without "sinning" then it is best not to marry at all. Notice their statement:

> *And I say to you, whoever divorces his wife, except for sexual immorality, and marries another, commits adultery; and whoever marries her who is divorced commits adultery." His disciples said to Him, "**If such is the case of the man with his wife, it is better not to marry**"* (Matt. 19:9-10).

14. Divorce and remarriage was very prevalent when Jesus was on earth as is also evidenced by the fact that the Samaritan woman had had five husbands.

> *The woman answered and said, "I have no husband." Jesus said to her, "You have well said, 'I have no husband,' for you have had **five husbands**, and the one whom you now have is not your husband; in that you spoke truly."* (John 4:17-18).

15. There is absolutely no question in my mind that the false teaching concerning "divorce" by the scribes and Pharisees is one of the reasons for the widespread sinful attitudes toward marriage and divorces among the Jews and those influenced by them in Jesus' day. This is the mindset that He was fighting while on earth and the reason for many of His statements about divorce and remarriage.

16. This is also the main reason that Jesus said on various occasions that everyone who "divorces" a faithful mate in

order to marry another "commits adultery" against their present mate. **These statements of Jesus were directed at the Pharisees because of their false teaching on the subject.** They were obviously saying something like, "It is not a sin to divorce your mate in order to marry someone else as long as you give her a certificate of divorce." But Jesus said, *"Whoever divorces his wife and marries another commits adultery against her"* (Mk. 10:11).

17. It is also interesting that on every occasion when Jesus discussed the subject of marital adultery, the Pharisees are mentioned in the context. Jesus only discussed the subject on four different occasions in the Gospels. Two times the Pharisees are mentioned in the context and two times they are directly responsible for the subject even coming up. The four times are as follows:

> In Matthew 5, the Pharisees are specifically mentioned in verse 20, and "adultery" is mentioned in verses 28, 31, and 32 of the same chapter.

> In Matthew 19, the Pharisees bring up the subject of divorce in verse 3 and Jesus speaks about "adultery" in verse 9.

> In Mark 10, the Pharisees again bring up the subject of divorce in verse 2 and Jesus teaches His disciples about "adultery" in verses 11 and 12.

> In Luke 16, the Pharisees are mentioned in verse 14 and Jesus teaches about marital adultery in verse 18.

18. There was actually a spiritual battle between Jesus and the Pharisees throughout His earthly ministry and we must keep this in mind when studying the subject of MDR.

Note: For more on this subject see Appendix number four: WHY IS UNDERSTANDING THE INFLUENCE AND TEACHING OF THE PHARISEES, ESPECIALLY IN THE BOOK OF MATTHEW, SO IMPORTANT IN THE MDR DISCUSSION?

16

What Did Jesus Teach About MDR?

1. We have already learned that Jesus taught basically the same thing that Moses did in Deuteronomy 24:1-4 about MDR.

2. Jesus only deals with the issue on four occasions. His teaching must be considered as a whole and not in an isolated verse.

3. One truth that we must keep in mind when studying any Bible subject is this: **Once a truth has been established on any subject that truth does not have to be repeated every time the subject comes up in order for it to be understood.** For example, Jesus taught us to baptize believers in the "name of the Father, and of the Son, and of the Holy Spirit" (Mt. 28:19). He only said that one time. But throughout the Book of Acts when believers were baptized, we know that it was in the name of the Father, Son, and Holy Spirit. Why? Because that truth was established in Matthew and should be understood every time water baptism is mentioned. Peter said that believers need to repent but that fact is not specifically

mentioned in Acts 8:12 or in some of the other conversion accounts in Acts, but it must be understood every time a conversion is mentioned because that truth was established in Luke 24:46-47 and Acts 2:38.

4. The same is true concerning what Jesus taught on MDR. What He taught in Matthew or Mark is to be automatically understood every time the subject comes up. This is an important point to keep in mind. For example, He only states "except for fornication" in Matthew's account. But that part is to be understood in Mark and Luke even though it is not specifically mentioned in either of those books. Also, He only states that divorcing a mate to marry someone else is committing adultery "against" the present mate in Mark's account. But that truth is to be understood when we read Matthew or Luke, even though neither one of them specifically mention that fact.

5. *It is also important to understand that Jesus was not dealing with all aspects of the MDR question during His earthly ministry.* For example, He is not dealing with marital abuse (Ex. 21:10-11; 1 Cor. 7:12ff), desertion (1 Cor. 7:15), or being unequally yoked in a marriage (2 Cor. 6:14ff). He is only dealing with divorcing in order to marry someone else. This is obviously what the Pharisees were doing and teaching and therefore this is the only aspect of the question that He is specifically addressing. The truth He taught is just as applicable to us as it was to them, but in order to understand how it applies to us or them, we must know what Jesus meant when He first said it.

6. For one to assume that this is all that Jesus said on the subject is not in accordance with the facts. Paul dealt with a number

of issues on the subject that the Lord Himself did not deal with (see 1 Corinthians 7:12ff). Many believers focus in on Matthew 19:9 and neglect or refuse to consider the other passages dealing with the same subject matter. It is interesting that we only do this on the MDR question. For example, in the Sermon on the Mount, Jesus teaches us to "swear not at all," "turn the other cheek," "give to him that asks," and "lend" to those who want to borrow. But we understand that all these statements must be interpreted or understood in light of all that is said in the New Testament and in light of the context where the statements are made. His teaching in the Sermon on the Mount is not to be isolated from other statements on the same subject. For example, we understand that we are not required to "give" or "lend" to those who will not work (2 Thess. 3:10) and we are not required to "turn the other cheek" when someone is breaking into our house (Mt. 24:43). We understand that Jesus is only dealing with certain aspects of these subjects and not dealing with these subjects in their entirety. But when it comes to MDR, we generally only know Matthew 5:31-32 and/or Matthew 19:1-9. We seem to think that this is all that is taught on the subject of MDR. But as with other subjects, these verses must be understood in light of the context as well as in light of the overall teaching on MDR. They are not to be isolated from the other verses relating to the same subject. Just remember that He is not dealing with all aspects of MDR in the four Gospels.

7. The four times Jesus referred to MDR, He was primarily discussing divorce and, more specifically, divorcing a faithful mate in order to marry someone else. The four times are as follows:

> *But I say to you that whoever divorces his wife*
> *for any reason except sexual immorality causes*

her to commit adultery; and whoever marries a woman who is divorced commits adultery (Mt. 5:32)

And I say to you, whoever divorces his wife, except for sexual immorality, and marries another, commits adultery; and whoever marries her who is divorced commits adultery (Mt. 19:9).

Whoever divorces his wife and marries another commits adultery against her. And if a woman divorces her husband and marries another, she commits adultery (Mk. 10:11-12).

Whoever divorces his wife and marries another commits adultery; and whoever marries her who is divorced from her husband commits adultery (Lk. 16:18).

8. The main point that Jesus is emphasizing in all of these passages is the sinfulness of breaking the marriage covenant by divorcing in order to remarry. Divorcing a faithful mate in order to marry someone else is sinful. Marrying a divorced person we have caused to be divorced is sinful. It is "committing adultery." The sinfulness of these acts cannot be challenged or denied.

9. When we put all that Jesus taught in these verses from the Gospel accounts together, adding what some writers leave out or do not mention, this is what we have: Whoever divorces his wife and marries someone else commits (marital) adultery *against her* when he does so, because he has broken the marriage covenant

he had with her through no fault of her own. Therefore, she is made to appear to commit adultery even though she is innocent. But if she has committed *fornication* and he divorces her and marries someone else he is not guilty of committing (marital) adultery against her because she is the one who broke the marriage covenant to marry someone else and not him. Also, whoever marries her who is put away *for fornication* is guilty of committing (marital) adultery along with her, *against* her former husband who put her away for *fornication,* because he is also responsible for breaking the marriage covenant she had with her husband who divorced her.

10. Notice what some today think Jesus is saying in Matthew 19:9:

> And I say to you, whoever divorces his wife, except for sexual immorality, and marries another, *does not* commit adultery *by divorcing in order to marry,* but **only** commits adultery *with his second wife when he has sex with her* and whoever marries her who is divorced *does not commit adultery by marrying her but* commits adultery *only when he has sex with her*.

OR

> And I say to you, whoever divorces his wife, except for sexual immorality, and marries another, *does not* commit adultery *by divorcing in order to marry.* But he *does* commit adultery *with his second wife when he has sex with her* and whoever marries her who is divorced *does*

not commit adultery by *marrying her* but commits adultery *only when he has sex with her*.

11. It is also important to understand that Jesus did not contradict what He later revealed through Paul in the letter to the Corinthians. In the Sermon on the Mount, Jesus clearly teaches that one who *divorces* a faithful mate in order to marry someone else is "committing adultery" against the mate he divorces. Keep in mind that the question that Jesus deals with in the Gospels is about "divorce" or "putting away" a marriage partner in order to marry someone else. This is clear in all of the gospel accounts:

*Whoever **divorces** his wife...* (Mt. 5:31).

*Whoever **divorces** his wife...* (Mt. 5:32).

*Is it lawful for a man to **divorce** his wife...* (Mt. 19:3).

*Why did Moses command to give a certificate of **divorce** and "put her away?"* (Mt. 19:7).

*Moses...permitted you to **divorce** your wives...* (Mt. 19:8).

*Whoever **divorces** his wife...* (Mt. 19:9).

*Is it lawful for a man to **divorce** his wife...* (Mk. 10:2).

*Whoever **divorces** his wife...* (Mk. 10:11).

*If a woman **divorces** her husband...* (Mk. 10:12).

*Whoever **divorces** his wife…* (Lk. 16:18).

12. Simply "marrying" another is not the main point. The main point is "divorcing" *in order* to marry another. If one divorces a faithful mate in order to marry someone else, he is committing adultery against his present mate when he does so. God has never permitted this. However, God has and does permit those who are divorced to marry. Jesus clearly revealed this through Paul.

13. Notice the apparent contradiction:

> Jesus said *"whoever marries her that is divorced commits adultery"* (Mt. 5:32).

> Paul said, *"are you loosed from a wife* (this includes the divorced) *… if you do marry, you have not sinned"* (1 Cor. 7:27-28).

14. In one instance Jesus says that to marry a divorced person is to "commit adultery." In another instance He inspires Paul to say that if you are divorced you can marry without sinning. How does that harmonize? The answer is, Jesus is dealing with *divorcing* or *causing a divorce* in order to marry and Paul is only dealing with *marrying*.

15. **It is not a sin for a divorced person to marry, but it is always a sin for a person to divorce a faithful mate or cause a mate to be divorced in order to marry.**

17

WHAT IS THE EXPLANATION
OF MATTHEW 19:1-9?

Now it came to pass, when Jesus had finished these sayings, that He departed from Galilee and came to the region of Judea beyond the Jordan. 2 And great multitudes followed Him, and He healed them there.3 The Pharisees also came to Him, testing Him, and saying to Him, "Is it lawful for a man to divorce his wife for just any reason?" 4 And He answered and said to them, "Have you not read that He who made them at the beginning 'made them male and female,' 5 and said, 'For this reason a man shall leave his father and mother and be joined to his wife, and the two shall become one flesh'? 6 So then, they are no longer two but one flesh. Therefore what God has joined together, let not man separate."7 They said to Him, "Why then did Moses command to give a certificate of divorce, and to put her away?"8 He said to them, "Moses, because of the hardness of your hearts, permitted you to divorce your wives, but from the beginning it was not so. 9 And I say to you, whoever divorces his wife, except for sexual immorality, and marries another, commits adultery; and whoever marries her who is divorced commits adultery."

1. In Matthew 19:1-9, the subject is divorce. But not *just* divorce. It is divorcing a mate in order to marry someone else, or causing a divorce in order to marry. This is the only issue Jesus is discussing (the same issue Jesus dealt with in Matthew 5:31-32.) He is not dealing with *all* aspects of the MDR question. In this context He is only dealing with what the Pharisees were teaching and/or practicing, and what they were asking Him about specifically.

2. We must keep in mind that Jesus is not addressing such issues as desertion or marital abuse or unequal yokes on this occasion. Those are all dealt with elsewhere, but not here.

3. The only question here is, "Is it lawful for a man to divorce his wife for just any reason and marry someone else?" This is what the Pharisees wanted to know. We know this is true because when Jesus answered the question, He included the subject of *remarriage* in the answer (Mt. 19:9). It was not just a question about divorce, but *divorcing in order to marry another*.

4. It is important first to focus on who is asking the question. It was not a faithful husband who had been deserted by his wife. It was not a faithful wife who was suffering domestic violence from an abusive husband. It was not a marriage partner whose mate was causing them to turn away from God. It was not a Samaritan woman seeking an honest answer (Jn. 4). It was not a woman caught in the act of adultery and needing forgiveness (Jn. 8). But it was the Pharisees. It was an "adulterous" group of religious leaders (Mt. 16:4) who wanted to "justify" what they were doing in divorcing and remarrying (Lk. 16:15-18). They were hypocritical leaders

who were full of sexual "uncleanness" (Mt. 23:27). *They were the ones asking the question* (His own disciples asked Him about it in Mark 10, but their question was in response to the question raised by the Pharisees). They were asking the question "testing" Him. They were seeking to justify what they were teaching and/or practicing (Lk. 16:14-18). They were not honest people sincerely seeking the truth. They were not hurting people needing help. They only wanted to test Him in order to accuse Him. This is the reason Jesus answered the question as He did. To apply the Lord's teaching on this occasion to any and every case of divorce and remarriage is a huge mistake in my judgment.

5. In answering their question Jesus told them that divorce was never in God's original plan. Jesus points out that since the beginning of time, God's ideal will had always been one man for one woman for life. Jesus emphasizes that from the beginning God wanted them to become one flesh (one family unit) for life and never separate or divorce (Mt. 19:4-6).

6. They wanted to know, *"Why did Moses command to give her a certificate of divorce and put her away?"* Jesus explained that Moses allowed divorce for "uncleanness" because of the hardness of the hearts of the Jews in his day. They were obviously mistreating their wives and divorcing them for any reason they chose, so God had to regulate their sinful conduct and stop them from divorcing for just any reason. He commanded them to "give her a bill of divorcement" and put her away if (and only if) they found some "uncleanness" in her.

7. It is important to understand that God did not allow them to break His marriage law for just any and every reason under the Law of Moses. Moses did not say that it was OK to divorce your wives as long as she is given the bill of divorcement. He said that if she was guilty of "uncleanness" then they could give her a certificate of divorce and put her away. Some seem to think that their divorcing their wives was sinful, but God Himself allowed them to "sin" because of the hardness of their hearts. As long as they gave her the "bill of divorcement" God would permit/sanction/approve/ tolerate their sinful conduct because they had hard hearts. This, to me, is foolishness. God did not (I repeat, did not) give in to their sinful conduct. He did not make their sin "OK" as long as they gave her a "bill of divorcement." When people reason (?) in this fashion, they make the same mistake that the Pharisees did in Matthew 19. Moses never approved of divorce for just any reason at all. He taught the same thing Jesus did about it. That is precisely the reason Jesus asked, *"What did Moses command you?"* (Mk. 10:3). He surely did not ask this question and then say that Moses did not know what he was talking about. Why ask them, *"What did Moses command you?"* if what Moses commanded did not apply?

8. The truth is that what Moses commanded *did* apply, which is precisely why Jesus brought it up in Mark's account. He would have most likely brought it up here in Matthew 19 if the Pharisees had not brought it up themselves.

9. Jesus reaffirmed what Moses taught in His answer. Here is His answer:

And I say to you, whoever divorces his wife, **except for sexual immorality**, *and marries another, commits adultery; and whoever marries her who is divorced commits adultery.* (Matt. 19:9)

10. A man who divorces his wife in order to marry someone else commits marital adultery *against* the wife he is married to (Mk. 10:11). But if the wife he is married to is guilty of "sexual immorality" then he does not commit marital adultery *against* her by divorcing her. When he divorces her for her unfaithfulness to the marriage covenant, then he is not guilty of marital adultery, but she is. All marital adultery involves divorce, but not all divorce involves marital adultery.

11. *"And whoever marries her who is divorced commits adultery."* This refers to the person who marries the one who is put away for "sexual immorality." Jesus adds "and whoever marries her" who is "put away" because of "sexual immorality" commits adultery because he is also responsible for breaking up the marriage covenant between a husband and wife. I believe that the reason Jesus said this is because the Pharisees, who were "adulterous" (Mt. 16:4) and full of (sexual) "uncleanness" (Mt. 23:27), were lusting in their hearts after other men's wives (Mt. 5:28) and committing fornication with other men's wives and causing them to be put away—thus becoming one with her in destroying the marriage covenant. The same thing happens in our world today. Therefore, whoever marries a woman that he has caused to be put away for fornication is guilty of "committing adultery" along with the woman. This "adultery" is committed against her former mate when he marries her because he is

as much responsible for breaking the "marriage covenant" she had with her husband as she is. He is said to "commit adultery" by marrying her because he was obviously the one that she committed sexual immorality with, thus causing her to be divorced from her husband.

12. I believe it is something like supporting one who does not teach the "doctrine of Christ." When one supports a false teacher, then he *"shares in his evil deeds."* (2 Jn. 1:9-11). In much the same way, a man who causes a wife to be divorced shares in her evil deed. Therefore, whoever marries her "commits adultery" because he shared in causing the divorce or breaking of the covenant she had with her husband.

13. Finally, notice that this verse speaks of one who "commits adultery." Nothing is said about "keeps on" committing adultery. It is something that is done once against the wife he divorces. There is not a standard translation that I have seen that renders it "keeps on" committing adultery. **As a matter of fact, he cannot "keep on" committing adultery against his ex-wife because he is no longer married to her!** He "commits (marital) adultery" *against* her when he divorces her in order to marry someone else, but he does not "keep on" committing adultery *against* her when she is no longer his wife. It is interesting that in "The Everlasting Gospel" translated by Hugo McCord, he says in 1 John 1:7 that the blood of Jesus *"keeps on cleansing"* us from all sin. But in Matthew 19:9 he does not translate it as "keeps on committing adultery." Why? It is because one cannot keep on committing adultery against a woman who is no longer his wife. Actually it is, *"And I say to you, whoever divorces* (not keeps on divorcing) *his wife, except for sexual immorality,*

and marries (not keeps on marrying) *another, commits adultery* (not keeps on committing adultery); *and whoever marries* (not keeps on marrying) *her who is divorced* (not keeps on divorcing) *commits adultery* (not keeps on committing adultery)."

14. Remember this point: **If people cannot keep a person "still married" to a mate who divorced him with the "invisible clamp" or the "mysterious mystical marriage magnet" theory, then they cannot make them "keep on committing adultery" against someone to whom they are not married.** The idea that one "keeps on committing adultery" with the woman he is married to is only possible if he is somehow still married to his wife who put him away. And that, in my judgment, is not possible. Read the chapter again on "Are Those Divorced Still Married in God's Sight?"

18

WHAT IS THE EXPLANATION OF MATTHEW 5:31-32?

"Furthermore it has been said, 'Whoever divorces his wife, let him give her a certificate of divorce.' But I say to you that whoever divorces his wife for any reason except sexual immorality causes her to commit adultery; and whoever marries a woman who is divorced commits adultery (Matt. 5:31-32).

1. The Pharisees taught part of what Moses taught, but not all. As the reading clearly shows, the Pharisees taught that all that is involved is to **give her a certificate of divorce and put her away. They conveniently left part of what Moses had said completely out.** Moses did not just say that a man could divorce his wife by giving her a "certificate of divorce" and sending her away. Moses said that if he found some *"uncleanness"* in her, he could justifiably put her away. Jesus explains that the husband who puts her away must do so because he has found some "sexual immorality" in her which is exactly what Moses had taught. Otherwise, he

causes it to appear that she has committed "uncleanness" or "sexual immorality" which is the only reason God gave for putting her away. Again—and this is very important to understand—by putting her away he causes it to appear that *she* has "broken the marriage covenant" and is guilty of "uncleanness" (or sexual immorality). See Deuteronomy 24:1-4.

2. As with the other subjects discussed in the Sermon on the Mount, the Pharisees had corrupted God's teaching on MDR. The Pharisees were teaching that a man could put away his faithful wife for just "any cause" as long as he gave her the "bill of divorcement." She did not have to be guilty of "uncleanness" like Moses actually said. "Just give her the bill...and you can divorce her at will." They obviously taught that a man *does not sin* by putting away his faithful wife in order to marry someone else. But Jesus said doing so "causes her" to "commit adultery" (in appearance), even though she is not guilty of doing anything wrong. He "makes her" commit adultery (NASB). By giving her a "bill of divorcement" and putting her away, he is implicating her in his adulterous schemes when she is not guilty of doing anything wrong.

3. The Old Testament (Ezek. 18:20) and the New (Jam. 1:14-15) teaches that we are not guilty of the sins that others commit, including those of our parents or marriage partners. The only way for him to "cause her to commit adultery" by putting her away is in appearance or the way it is perceived. He is the guilty one, not her. It says nothing about her remarrying (even though that is possible and even likely). Read exactly what is actually said: *"whoever divorces his wife for any reason except sexual immorality causes her to commit*

adultery." Nothing else is necessary for her to do so. Nothing is said in this statement about her remarrying someone else. She did not do anything other than be the victim of a treacherous partner who put her away for no other reason than he wanted to marry someone else. The sin that Jesus is condemning is the sin of the person who is divorcing a faithful mate in order to marry someone else. He makes her appear to "commit adultery" by what he did to her, not by anything she did or will do. Jesus is not condemning the woman.

4. Foy Wallace, Jr. wrote:

*The language of the Lord teaches that when a man had put away his wife with reference to post-nuptial fornication, he was guilty of ignoring the marriage bond, and made an adulteress of an innocent wife **in appearance** when she was not an adulteress in fact. Where the King James text reads, "causeth her to commit adultery," the American Standard text puts it, "maketh her an adulteress." She is made an adulteress, when she is not, in the same sense of 2 Corinthians 5:21 where it is said of Christ that "him who knew no sin was made to be sin." **The text does not say that she becomes an adulteress, but that she is made an adulteress**"* (emphasis supplied). (The Sermon on the Mount and the Civil State, pg. 40).

5. Some will possibly object to understanding that the "adultery" is only in "appearance" and not in actual fact. But it seems obvious that this is the only way she can be "caused" or "made" to commit adultery when she is divorced. Notice that Jesus says *"whoever divorces his wife...causes her to commit adultery."* Read it again: whoever "divorces" his wife "causes her" to "commit adultery." Divorcing her "causes

her" to "commit adultery." The only way that is possible is in the way it *appears* and not the way it actually is. He cannot possibly cause her to commit adultery in actual fact by divorcing her. The text does not say that she "becomes" an adulteress *when* she marries someone else, but he "makes her" (NASB) commit adultery by divorcing her. Hugo McCord translates it *"leaves her debased."* (The Everlasting Gospel, Mt. 5:32). Debased means ruined in character or quality. This is the way it appears by the way she is treated. Her character in the eyes of others is adversely affected by what he did to her! Suppose for example that a highly respected religious leader were to divorce his wife. What would some people automatically think? They would most likely think that she had been unfaithful. He would actually "cause her" to be considered unfaithful to the marriage covenant in some way, even though she may be totally innocent.

6. Those who might object to the understanding that it is only in "appearance" and not in actual fact that she is caused to "commit adultery" must add numerous things that are not in the text to believe what they believe in most cases. For example, some believe that she commits adultery only *when* she remarries someone else. But there is nothing in the text about this. Nothing! Read it. Read it again. *Absolutely nothing is said about her remarrying.* One more time, whoever "divorces" his wife "causes her" to "commit adultery." She is caused to commit adultery by what he did to her, not by what she does herself. What if she never marries someone else? Jesus does not say he "causes her to commit adultery *when she marries someone else.*" He said he causes her to commit adultery by divorcing her. This popular view would actually contradict what Jesus said if she did not remarry.

This view would have Jesus saying: "Whoever divorces his wife for any reason except sexual immorality does not cause her to commit adultery unless she remarries." And even then that is not enough "addition" for some. They would have to add the following: Whoever divorces his wife for any reason except sexual immorality *does not* cause her to commit adultery *unless she remarries* and *even then she will only* commit adultery *when she has sex with her new husband*. I personally believe that it is just as Jesus said. Read it again: *"whoever divorces his wife for any reason except sexual immorality causes her to commit adultery."* And that statement is true every time it happens, whether she remarries or not. But it is only in *appearance* and not in actual fact.

7. In order to help you better understand the meaning of "causes her to commit adultery" think about the following comparison. Suppose that the law of our land said, "Whoever murders someone shall be surely put to death in the electric chair." If we were to read in the newspaper that someone was executed in the electric chair, we would automatically assume they had murdered someone. It would appear to us that they were guilty. But what if they were really innocent but no one knew it? They would still be guilty of murder in the eyes of those in the country—but only in appearance.

8. When Jesus was crucified the Jews and Romans "caused Him to be a criminal" in appearance. It *appeared* that He was a criminal like the thieves who were crucified with Him because the Romans crucified criminals. But He was only a criminal in appearance. *"Yet we esteemed Him stricken, smitten by God, and afflicted"* for His own sins (Isa. 53:4b). This is the way it "appeared" but not the way it was. Jesus

was "innocent" of sin, but He was made to "appear" to be guilty because He was treated as one guilty would be treated. The same is true of an "innocent" woman who is put away like one who is guilty.

9. Jesus adds, "and whoever marries one" who is "put away" because of "uncleanness" or "sexual immorality" is committing adultery because he is also responsible for breaking up the marriage covenant between a husband and wife. I believe that the reason Jesus said this is because the Pharisees, who were "adulterous" (Mt. 16:4) and full of sexual "uncleanness" (Mt. 23:27), were lusting in their hearts after other men's wives (Mt. 5:28) and committing fornication with other men's wives, causing them to be put away—thus destroying the marriage covenant. The same thing happens in our world today. Therefore, whoever marries a woman that he has caused to be put away for fornication is guilty of "committing adultery" along with her against her former mate when he marries her. He is as responsible as she is for breaking the "marriage covenant" she had with her husband.

10. It is important to understand that marital adultery is committed "against" a marriage partner and not *with* a marriage partner (Mk. 10:11).

11. Note that it is not the sex in the marriage to the second partner that constitutes the "adultery," but putting away (breaking a covenant with) the mate you are married to *in order to marry another*. This is what constitutes marital adultery. I am not married to the second mate when I "divorce" my first mate. Therefore, the adultery must be committed "while I am still married" to my wife in order for it to be

"against her." If she is already put away and I am no longer her husband, then I cannot be committing adultery "against" her by marrying someone else. But if I put her away *while* she is still married to me in order to marry someone else, then the adultery is indeed "against her."

12. Note: **The only way to make the adultery occur when he has sex with his new wife is for the humanly devised "imaginary clamp" to be in place — which it is not.** I have already proven earlier in this book, that the man-made "mysterious mystical marriage magnet" that supposedly keeps two people married to each other who are divorced from each other is not only obviously missing, but it never existed in the first place.

13. Another point on this matter is that Jesus does not say he "causes her to commit adultery *when she marries someone else.*" As a matter of fact, a woman who is put away does not sin when she marries. Paul clearly states that a woman who is "loosed from" (divorced) does not sin by getting married (1 Cor. 7:27-28). The only way for this not to be true is for her to still be bound to her husband and that is simply not the case as has been demonstrated in this book. So He cannot be saying that she commits adultery "when she marries someone else" or when she has sex with her new husband.

14. One final point is that God is surely not more merciful, when it comes to remarrying, to a "woman" who is deserted (1 Cor. 7:15) than He is to a woman who is put away unjustly (Matt. 5:32). Neither of them is guilty of anything that destroyed the marriage. One is unjustly "deserted" and one is unjustly "put away." But some believe that the one

deserted is allowed to remarry without sinning but the other who is unjustly put away "commits adultery" by marrying. They believe that the woman deserted is not under bondage to the marriage, but the woman unjustly put away is still in bondage to the marriage. I personally do not believe that that could possibly be true.

19

WHO IS AUTHORIZED TO MARRY?

1. When it comes to who is eligible to marry, some would give a list of three (and only three) categories. This is a list comprised by uninspired men who are quite obviously uninformed. Many preachers keep insisting on this list, but the verses teaching or even implying it are missing. The three groups who are eligible to marry, according to some, are:

> a. Those that have never been married.

> b. Those that have divorced their spouses because their spouses committed fornication.

> c. Those whose spouses have died.

2. Is this what the Bible teaches? Absolutely not! The Bible clearly teaches that those who have never been married and those who are now "loosed from" a wife (including the divorced) can get married if they need to and want to.

*Are you bound to a wife? Do not seek to be loosed. **Are you loosed from a wife?** Do not seek a wife. But even **if you do marry**, you have **not sinned**; and if a virgin marries, she has not sinned.* (1 Corinthians 7:27-28).

3. It is quite clear that when Paul asks, *"Are you bound to a wife?"* that he is asking "are you *married* to a wife?" If one is bound "to" a wife, he is obviously married to her. When he asks, *"Are you loosed from a wife?"* he is asking "are you *divorced* from a wife?" If one is loosed "from" a wife, he is obviously divorced from her. Strong's Concordance says the word "loosed" means a loosing of the bond of marriage or divorced.

4. In these verses, Paul plainly says that if a "virgin" (one who has never married) marries, she has "not sinned." He is also just as clear in saying that if one is "loosed from (divorced from)" a wife, they have "not sinned" if they marry.

5. It does not matter how or why one is "loosed from" a mate; if they marry they have not sinned. Whether one is "loosed from" the marriage bond by God's law of putting one away because of "fornication," or by God's law concerning being "deserted," or by God's law concerning the death of a spouse, or whether they are "loosed" contrary to what God has said—if they are "loosed" from a wife for whatever reason, if they marry, they have not sinned. Marrying is not a sin, but *divorcing* a faithful mate in order to marry another is.

6. How or why they became "loosed" or divorced is not discussed in 1 Corinthians 7:27-28. **There is no doubt that**

**many in the church at Corinth had been divorced for
various reasons (authorized and unauthorized), but they
were "loosed" and therefore, if they did "marry" they
had "not sinned."**

7. What we must understand is that marriage is an "honorable" relationship for everyone. It is an "honorable" relationship to be in. Hebrews 13:4 says, *"Marriage is **honorable
among all**, and the bed undefiled; but fornicators and adulterers God will judge."* It is an honorable state for "all."

8. In order for one to avoid fornication (sexual immorality/
sex outside marriage), each one is to be married. Because
of the temptation to commit sexual sins, all of those who
are tempted need to get married. *"Nevertheless, because of
sexual immorality, let each man have his own wife, and let
each woman have her own husband"* (1 Cor. 7:2). It is far
better for one to marry and be in a legitimate relationship
than to burn with sexual passion. This applies to anyone who
does not have self-control in the area of sexual temptation—
which applies to most people. *"But if they cannot exercise
self-control, let them marry. For it is better to marry than to
burn with passion."* (1 Cor. 7:9)

9. The thing that we must realize and get clear in our minds
is that marriage is an honorable state or relationship in which
to be. It is true that "how" we got into that state may have
been sinful, but being in a "married state/relationship" is not
sinful. Observe the following points.

10. Being "single" is an "honorable state/condition" in which
to be. But how one got to be single may not have been in

116

an honorable way or the right thing to do. Paul instructed two believers to stay married. But he also said that if they divorced, they should *"remain unmarried"* (1 Cor. 7:10-11). Why could they "remain unmarried" (stay single)? Because there is nothing wrong with being in a single state or condition. It is wrong to "depart" from a mate, but it is not wrong to be single or "unmarried."

11. Being a mother is an "honorable state" in which to be. There is nothing wrong with being a mother in a relationship with her children. But the way some females *become* mothers is sinful. If, for example, a young unmarried girl gets pregnant by her boyfriend and has a baby, she is a mother. And there is nothing wrong with her being a mother, but how she *became* a mother was and is wrong.

12. Being married is an "honorable state/condition/relationship" in which to be. There is nothing wrong with being "married." But how some got to be married was wrong. There was obviously nothing wrong with David being "married" to Bathsheba. Solomon and Jesus were both born as a result of that marriage (Matt. 1:6-16). But the way their marriage came about was both shameful and sinful. The same is true of many marriages today. They came about as a result of shame and sin, but being in a "married state" or relationship is not sin. **Therefore, those who are remarried not only should not divorce, they *must* not.**

13. According to Paul, those "loosed" from a mate have "not sinned" if they marry (1 Cor. 7:27-28). When the Holy Spirit plainly says that those "loosed from" a mate do not sin in getting married, then all of the "human" spirits in the

world cannot change that truth. The inspired man said that if one is "loosed from" a wife, if they marry, they have "not sinned." If we let uninspired men tell us otherwise, then we can believe what we please.

14. **Furthermore, we have no right to bind celibacy on those who are not gifted to live celibate lives.** For example, binding celibacy on those not "gifted" to be celibate is not only unscriptural, it is also unnatural. Paul clearly taught that all are not able to live celibate lives.

*"For I would that all men were even as I myself. But every man hath his proper **gift** of God, one after this manner, and another after that"* (1 Cor. 7:7).

15. Observe that Paul said the ability to live single is a "gift" from God. And even though he *desired* that all believers were single like he was, he did not *demand* that they be single like he was.

16. Jesus also taught that all men do not need to marry, because there are some who are eunuchs and have no need of marriage.

> *But He said to them, "**All cannot accept this saying,** but only those to whom it has been given: For there are eunuchs who were born thus from their mother's womb, and there are eunuchs who were made eunuchs by men, and there are eunuchs who have made themselves eunuchs for the kingdom of heaven's sake. He*

who is able to accept it, let him accept it" (Matt. 19:11-12).

17. Observe that Jesus said that there are some who are "eunuchs" and have no need to be married. Some were born that way, some were made that way by others (castration, etc), and some have "made themselves eunuchs" for the sake of the kingdom of God. These last ones obviously "made themselves eunuchs" because the "gift" of celibacy had been given to them by God. **It is right and proper for one to make themselves celibate if they have that "gift," but that does not give preachers, elders, and others the right to demand that people live celibate lives that do not have the gift!**

18. There is no statement in the Bible about two divorced single people who marry being in an "adulterous marriage" or "living in adultery" with their spouse or being in "unscriptural marriages." The circumstances that brought about some marriages are less than ideal and many times sinful, but being in the marriage relationship itself is not a sin.

20

CAN A PERSON "LIVE IN ADULTERY"?

1. Is it possible to "live in adultery"? Yes! One way to "live in adultery" is for one to "marry" someone who is still married to a husband. Paul makes that clear in Romans 7:1-3 when he writes:

> *Or do you not know, brethren (for I speak to those who know the law), that the law has dominion over a man as long as he lives? For the woman who has a husband is bound by the law to her husband as long as he lives. But if the husband dies, she is released from the law of her husband. So then if, **while her husband lives, she marries another man**, she will be called an **adulteress**; but if her husband dies, she is free from that law, so that she is no adulteress, though she has married another man.*

2. I believe that such a woman would be "living in an adulterous relationship" and, therefore, would be an "adulteress"

as long as she stayed/continued/remained in that state or relationship.

3. This was one of the problems with Herod being "married" to Herodias. She was not a widow nor was she divorced from Philip according to the Law of Moses (Deut. 24:1-4). She is always referred to as "Philip's wife" (Mt. 14:3; Mk. 6:17-18; Lk. 3:19). There is absolutely no proof that she was given the "bill of divorcement" and sent away from Philip like the Law of Moses said. Furthermore, this was a case of incest, which was forbidden by Moses (Lev. 18:16), as well as adultery. She was "living in adultery," not because she was divorced and then remarried (like those in our discussion), but because she was "married" to Philip at the same time that she "married" Herod. Her husband was living and she was still married to him, but was now also married to another man, which according to the law of marriage made her an "adulteress." It was not lawful for him to have his brother Philip's wife (Mk. 6:17-18).

4. I also believe that if a man (married or single) had an "ongoing" affair (sexual relationship) with a married woman, that he would be "living in adultery" in that sense.

5. The Bible does teach that those who once "walked" (continued as a way of life) in sin (sexual and otherwise) are those who "lived in them."

> *Therefore put to death your members which are*
> *on the earth: fornication, uncleanness, passion,*
> *evil desire, and covetousness, which is idolatry.*
> *Because of these things the wrath of God is*

*coming upon the sons of disobedience, in which
you yourselves **once walked** when you **lived in
them**.* (Col 3:5-7).

6. Observe that he mentions "fornication" (which could
include adultery) as well as other sins, and said that they "once
walked" in these sins, and therefore they "lived in them."

7. So I believe the Bible teaches that it is possible for one to
"live in" an adulterous state or ongoing adulterous relationship and, in that sense, they would be "living in adultery."

8. However, I do not believe that a man can "live in adultery"
with one to whom he is *legitimately married*. He cannot "live
in adultery" if he is faithful to his wife. As we have already
pointed out, those who have never married and those "loosed
(divorced) from a wife" can marry and they have "not sinned"
by marrying (1 Cor. 7:27-28). Since they have "not sinned"
by *getting* married, then they obviously do not sin in *staying*
married. The main point that we must continually remember
is that "marriage" is an honorable relationship, regardless of
the circumstances (favorable or unfavorable) that made the
marriage possible. As long as a man and woman legitimately
enter a "marriage covenant," and remain faithful to it, they
do not and cannot "live in adultery" with each other.

21

CAN THE GUILTY PERSON WHO IS PUT AWAY BECAUSE OF FORNICATION MARRY SOMEONE ELSE?

1. Special Note: Nothing that is written in this chapter should be interpreted as encouraging or endorsing the breaking of the marriage covenant with a faithful spouse. This chapter is about *pardon* for those who have sinned, and not about *permission* for those who want to sin. It is about *forgiveness* of sin, and not about *freedom* to sin. Divorcing a faithful spouse, especially in order to marry someone else, is always wrong no matter who does it. God has always "hated" divorcing faithful companions and those who do so sin, not only against their *mate* but more importantly against their *Maker*! Divorcing a faithful mate, especially in order to marry someone, is sinful — period. In doing so, one "commits adultery" against the faithful spouse (Mk. 10:11). It is treacherous! It is faithless. It is condemned in no uncertain terms both in the Old Testament and the New (see Malachi

2:13-16; Matthew 19:1-9). If you are now married to a faithful spouse (whether first, second, or fifth) God says that you are to stay married.

2. But the question is: Can a man (and the same would be true of a woman) who has been guilty of "sexual immorality" (Matt. 19:9, NKJV) or "fornication" (KJV) and who has already been "put away" (divorced) be forgiven of that sin? Can he later marry someone else without sinning? In other words, can a man who has been divorced by a mate because he has been guilty of adultery then later marry someone else without being guilty of sin when he does so? Does he have a right to be married to another person? Does God recognize/approve/sanction the marriage to the other person? Will he be married in "God's sight" to his new wife?

3. The Bible answer to all of these questions is: YES! Of course he can be forgiven if he repents and seeks forgiveness. And yes he can marry again. According to Jesus, when a person is "put away" because of fornication (KJV) or sexual immorality (NKJV) he is "put away" (Matthew 19:9). He is not "partly" put away, or "nearly" put away, or "somewhat" put away, or "almost" put away—He is "put away." He is divorced and the marriage is formally terminated, totally and completely. That means that he is not still married to her in any sense. He is not married in man's sight. He is not married in God's sight. And he is not married in anybody's sight that can see things as they are! Most all agree that the wife who put him away is free to marry someone else because she put him away because of his fornication. But if she is free from that marriage and, therefore, no longer married to him, then *he is no longer married to her*. Both are *unmarried* after the

divorce. The idea that the "guilty party" is somehow still bound to the woman who divorced him, or that he is bound by some "mystical magnet" or "invisible clamp" or to some (unknown) "law of God demanding his celibacy," is not only wrong and unscriptural, it is downright ludicrous. One mate cannot be free from a marriage and the other mate still be bound by that marriage. The idea that "she" is *not* married to "him," but he is somehow still "married to her" in *some* sense, makes absolutely *no* sense! In fact, it is *nonsense*! There is no "invisible clamp" that God places on a "marriage covenant" that cannot be broken if they divorce. If they are divorced then they are both "unmarried."

4. The question then is: Can a person who has been "loosed from" or "released from" (divorced from) a wife marry someone else without sinning? Read the answer from the Bible for yourself. It is in 1 Corinthians 7:27-28:

> *Are you bound to a wife? Do not seek to be loosed. Are you **loosed from** a wife? Do not seek a wife. But even if you **do marry**, you have **not sinned**; and if a virgin marries, she has not sinned. Nevertheless such will have trouble in the flesh, but I would spare you.*

> *Are you bound to a wife? Do not seek to be released. Are you **released from** a wife? Do not seek a wife. But **if you marry**, you have **not sinned**; and if a virgin marries, she has not sinned. Yet such will have trouble in this life, and I am trying to spare you.* (New American Standard Bible)

5. Notice carefully that the Bible clearly says if you have been "loosed" or "released" (divorced), and are therefore unmarried and do not have a wife, then "if you do marry, you have *not* sinned." Why is that the case with the one who is guilty of unfaithfulness in a divorce for fornication or adultery? *It is because he no longer has a wife.* He has been "put away" and is, therefore, "unmarried." The marriage to his first wife is as though it never happened. His former wife is totally free from that marriage because she "put him away," and he is totally free from that marriage relationship because he has *been* "put away." **It would be impossible for him to still be married to her, but her to not be married to him. If she is free from the marriage, then he is as free as she is. There is no possible way that he can "commit adultery** *against her*" **(Mark 10:11) when he remarries, because she is not his wife and he is not her husband.** He has been "put way."

6. Another thing that needs to be pointed out is that Jesus did not contradict Moses on this subject. He did not change what Moses said about it (Matthew 5:1-20). In fact, He upheld what Moses taught. In Deuteronomy 24:1-4, Moses wrote:

> *When a man takes a wife and marries her, and it happens that she finds no favor in his eyes* ***because he has found some uncleanness in her***, *and he writes her a certificate of divorce, puts it in her hand, and sends her out of his house, when she has departed from his house,* ***and goes and becomes another man's wife,.....***

7. Observe that Moses taught that the one guilty of "uncleanness" could go out and marry and when she does she "becomes another man's wife." Even though she was "guilty" of "uncleanness," she was nevertheless free to remarry because she had been properly and formally divorced.

8. Jesus taught the same thing but He used the words "sexual immorality" instead of "uncleanness." (Matt. 19:9). In doing so, He was actually explaining what kind of "uncleanness" to which Moses was referring.

9. Jesus said in Matthew 5:32 and Matthew 19:9 that in a case where the marriage ends because of fornication, the "one flesh" relationship is over—totally and completely. Therefore, both parties (the innocent and the one guilty of fornication) in a divorce because of fornication (or adultery) are free to remarry someone else without sinning when they do.

10. God "hates divorce" in such cases (Malachi 2:13-16). But these things happen. Those who sin in ending marriages in an unscriptural way should repent and seek forgiveness. But there is nothing they can do about the past. What's done is done! A person who has believed and been baptized is forgiven of all sin (Mk. 16:16), including marital unfaithfulness. A Christian, who has repented and confessed, has been forgiven of all sin, including marital unfaithfulness (1 John 1:9).

11. David was forgiven of this very sin (2 Samuel 11, 12; Psalm 51, 32). Those today that deliberately violate God's marriage law can also be forgiven just as David was when they repent and seek God's forgiveness. *Acceptance* of those who have committed this sin is not an *approval* of the sin

that they have committed. God certainly did not approve of David's sin with Bathsheba and David suffered for it, but He forgave David and blessed him in his subsequent marriage to her.

12. Paul committed many sins, including murder, which most of us have not done. But he said that he was *"forgetting those things that are behind"* (past mistakes, sins, and bad decisions), and *"reaching forward to those things which are ahead"* (Phil. 3:6-13). Paul refused to live in the past and so should the rest of us. In First Corinthians 6:9-11, Paul said that some in the church in Corinth had been very sinful. Some of them had been "fornicators" and "adulterers" in the past but, having been forgiven, they were "washed," "sanctified," and "justified" by the power (in the name) of the Lord Jesus and by the Spirit of God. This is what knowing Jesus and the salvation that He freely gives us is all about!

13. *Forgiveness is for those who have failed, not for those who are faultless.*

Note: For more on this point see Appendix number five: WHAT HAVE OTHERS SAID ABOUT THE GUILTY PARTY REMARRYING?

22

HOW DOES ONE REPENT
OF MARITAL ADULTERY?

1. A person repents of marital adultery by changing his mind about it, which results in a change of action. When a person turns to Jesus for forgiveness, he decides to stop divorcing and remarrying and decides to remain faithful to his mate to whom he is married. If he is married to his second wife, he is to stay married to her.

2. He certainly does not repent of "divorcing a faithful mate" by divorcing his present faithful mate. A person does not repent of murder by murdering someone else. A girl does not repent of having a child outside of marriage by having another child outside of marriage or by aborting the child.

3. Since when does repenting of a sin demand that we commit the same sin again? If divorcing a faithful mate is wrong, it is wrong every time it is done. Surely a person who has "committed adultery" against a mate in the past by divorcing her/him to marry someone else does not have to "commit adultery" again by divorcing the one he/she is married to in order

to marry someone else. One does not repent of "committing (marital) adultery" by "committing (marital) adultery."

4. David repented of the adultery with Bathsheba, not by divorcing her, but by deciding to stop doing what he had done in the past. He maintained his marital relationship with her, even though he was sorry about how the marriage came about.

5. When one repents of conceiving a child out of wedlock, they do not have to abort the child or give up the child. They simply decide not to do the same thing again and they maintain the family relationship.

6. The same is true of sins against marriage. A person does not have to divorce a faithful companion in order to repent of a sin committed in the past. It is true that some marriages came about as a result of sin, but being in a marriage relationship is not a sin—whether it is a first, second, or subsequent marriage.

7. *Those that encourage or require married people to divorce their mates are causing them to do something God hates* (Mal. 2:16). There should be a very clear example in the New Testament of married people being made to divorce if we are to partake in such a thing, but there is not. No one in the New Testament church was ever commanded to divorce their present faithful mate for any reason. It is both a presumptuous and preposterous practice. **Divorcing a faithful mate is always sinful, even when preachers and church leaders encourage or require it.**

23

What About "Profiting" From Sin?

1. If the "guilty party" in a divorce may keep their new mate, then are they not "profiting" from their sin? Yes! Remarriage after an unlawful divorce can be viewed as "profiting" from sin in a sense, especially if one is happily married to his/her new wife/husband. Likewise a single girl who gets pregnant and has a child that she loves "profits" from her sin in that same sense. She has a child that she loves and will in most cases "profit" a lot from that relationship over the years. But this does not make the sin right or the new relationship with her child wrong. The mother/child relationship is a legitimate relationship and one that should not be taken lightly and certainly not condemned. The way the relationship came about in those cases was sinful, but the relationship itself is not. Furthermore, the fact that she enjoys this new relationship and would not change it if she could does not make how it came about right or any less sinful.

2. It is the same way with the marriage relationship. Marriage is an honorable relationship. It is "honorable in all" (Heb.

13:4). But the way some marriages come about is both sinful and shameful. David's marriage to Bathsheba was an honorable relationship. They were blessed with Solomon and other sons. Jesus was born in that lineage (Matt. 1:6). But the way their marriage relationship came about was about as sinful as could be.

3. Joseph's brothers "profited" from their sin against Joseph in the sense that their lives were saved and they enjoyed some of the best land in Egypt. They received numerous other benefits as a result of their sin against him, but that does not make jealousy, mistreating him, and selling him into slavery any less sinful or wicked.

4. The Jews who crucified Jesus "profited" from that sin in one sense because killing Jesus is how they obtained forgiveness. (Just so you know, the same is true of all of us. Our sins killed Jesus and in that sense we all "profit" from our own sins). But that does not make the sin that is committed right or the act justified. It was "lawless hands" that crucified Jesus (Acts 2:23). But it is with "His stripes" (that were administered by those lawless hands) that we are "healed" or by which we "profit" if you want to look at it that way (Isa. 53:5).

5. The problem with this kind of reasoning (?) is that it fails to look at the big picture. We only see a person, who obviously sinned, with a new mate now enjoying the new relationship. But there is more to it than that. For one to think that people who commit adultery get off totally free is simply not true. As a matter of fact, no one "gets away" with any

sin. **All sin is punished no matter what the sin is or who does the sinning.**

6. For example, a point that is often overlooked is the fact that no unlawful divorce goes without being punished. We believe that those who deal treacherously by destroying the marriages of innocent mates deserve to be punished. And they do! And they will suffer eternal punishment because of it! You can count on it! The wages of sin is death and it will happen (Rom. 6:23). The law of sowing and reaping guarantees it (Gal. 6:7-9). Unless!...Unless!...Unless they turn to Jesus for mercy and forgiveness and allow Him to pay the penalty for the sin. Then, like the rest of us who have sinned in other ways, there is His *forgiveness*. He suffered the punishment for David and his marital sins and He will do it for any others who repent and seek His forgiveness like David did. *But no sin goes unpunished!*

7. Another thing that is often overlooked is the matter of chastisement. God disciplines His children who violate His will (Heb. 12:5-11). Joseph's brothers suffered the consequences of guilty consciences and other adverse effects of their sin when we look at it from the other side of the coin. David's child died and there were problems in his family as a result/consequence of his sin with Bathsheba (2 Sam. 12). Women who have children out of wedlock must suffer some negative effects of that sin and there are always some negative effects. In the same way, those responsible for destroying marriages, whether Christian or not, usually suffer some undesirable consequences of that sin. Personally, I have never met a person in this situation who did not suffer some negative effects of their sin. **But it is God's business to deal**

with how He disciplines in those situations and certainly not ours. If He had wanted us involved He would have told us plainly what to do and not left it for us to "figure" out. Destroying established families is serious business especially since God did not tell us to do it nor did He give us an example of it being done anywhere in the New Testament!

8. The thing that we must realize is that those who are guilty of "marital adultery" need mercy just like everybody else who has sinned. Mercy is "not getting what they deserve." It is interesting that when David sought forgiveness for his adultery and murder, the first thing that he said in his prayer of repentance was, *"Have **mercy** upon me, O God, according to Your lovingkindness. according to the multitude of Your tender **mercies**"* (Ps. 51:1-2). He threw himself on the mercy of God, so to speak. This is exactly what those guilty of marital adultery need to do today. Without God's mercy, they are doomed just like the rest of us.

9. Psalm 136 is one of the most unusual chapters in the Bible. It has twenty-six verses. But that is not what makes it unusual. There are plenty of chapters in the Bible that have at least twenty-six verses. The thing that makes it unusual is the fact that all twenty-six verses end with the same phrase. Know what it is? Here it is: *"For His mercy endures forever."* Time after time after time. Twenty-six times in a row, *"For His mercy endures forever."* This truth needs to sink in when it comes to those who have made marriage mistakes and been guilty of marital adultery. God has mercy for them just like He does for all others who sin. He has not used it up. He has not run out of it. It was not just for David and his

marital sins. The "gift of God" is not just for the Samaritan woman (who had had five husbands) and her marital sins. His mercy endures forever. It not only *endures* but it also *cures*. God forgives the sin of the person guilty of adultery who sincerely seeks forgiveness.

10. Another point that needs to be cleared up is the idea that we believe all one has to do once they have committed marital adultery against a mate is just *say 'I'm sorry' and go on their merry way* in the new relationship. The very use of this language is designed to prejudice the reader against the conclusion that those guilty of destroying marriages can be forgiven and can remarry after being divorced.

11. For example, since when did just *saying* "I'm sorry" constitute repentance? Try that with other sins.

> All one has to do to be forgiven of "lying" is just say "I'm sorry" and go on their merry way.

> All one has to do to be forgiven of "murder" is just say "I'm sorry" and go on their merry way.

> All a young man has to do to be forgiven for getting his girlfriend pregnant is just say "I'm sorry" and go on his merry way.

> Or, all one has to do to be forgiven for being unconcerned and "unmerciful" to those involved in MDR is just say "I'm sorry" and go on their merry way.

12. See what I mean! Just saying "I'm sorry" with no real "godly sorrow" for the sin will not lead to repentance or salvation from any sin—marital or otherwise. Paul wrote, *"For godly sorrow produces repentance leading to salvation, not to be regretted; but the sorrow of the world produces death"* (2 Cor. 7:10).

13. Godly sorrow involves actually "being" sorry that God's marriage law was violated and fornication was committed. It is actually "being" sorry to the point of deciding to seek forgiveness from God and making a conscious decision not to commit fornication and/or marital adultery again. This means that the guilty one determines, "I am not going to commit fornication or divorce my wife/husband in order to marry someone else ever again. I have really/actually/ honestly changed my mind and therefore repented of that mind set."

14. If you really want to understand what repentance and being sorry for committing adultery really involves, read Psalm 51, David's prayer of repentance. He did not just "say" he was sorry. It was not some flippant attitude of getting away with something. He was remorseful! He was actually sorry for sinning against God! This is the same attitude of many today who have sinned against a marriage companion. And they can be forgiven and go on with their lives, even in a new relationship, just as David did. Furthermore, they can even use what they did and what has happened to them to teach others about repentance and forgiveness, and sinners can be converted. According to Psalm 51:12-13 this is exactly what David did.

15. But we still wonder how one can repent of fornication and destroying a marriage by that sin and yet stay in a marriage relationship with a new mate that is a result of that sin. **The answer is that the fornication and destroying the marriage was sin, but the new marriage relationship created as a result of that sin is not sinful. It is not sinful to be married.** Marriage is an honorable relationship. But how can one stay in a relationship that came about as a result of sin? The answer to this is:

> In the same way a girl who gets pregnant by committing fornication can remain in the relationship with her child. Committing fornication is sinful, but the relationship created by the sin is not sinful.

> In the same way churches that split because of sin can later repent of the sin committed in splitting the church and still maintain and continue in separate congregations. Dividing a church is sinful, but maintaining a relationship in the new congregation is not sinful. (If repentance demanded getting back with the one they split from, most congregations I know in our area would have to disband...including where I am!).

> In the same way a young man and woman can have sex and she gets pregnant and they marry as a direct result of that sin. The way the marriage came about was sinful, but the marriage relationship that was created is not sinful.

In the same way one in a divorce can remain single. The way he/she became single by divorcing is wrong, but being in a single state is not wrong (1 Cor. 7:10-11).

In the same way a widow who does not marry "in the Lord" can remain in that marriage (1 Cor. 7:39). The way she entered the marriage was sinful if she did not marry "in the Lord," but the relationship of being married is not sinful. Who would demand that she divorce her husband? (I should not have asked that question. Since there are still some who insist on breaking up established families, leaving children without one parent in the home, or who refuse to baptize/fellowship some involved in MDR, they would most likely have no trouble demanding that a "widow" divorce her husband!)

In the same way David could stay in a marriage with Bathsheba that came about as a result of them both being involved in sin.

16. The thing that we must constantly keep in mind is that married people sometimes fall (or jump) into sin. If David (a man after God's own heart) could get caught up in this sin, then anybody can. This is especially true of those who do not even know the Lord or anything about Him. Those married people in the world many times are involved in MDR and do not even know that what they have done is wrong and don't care! But it is wrong! And when they hear the gospel of Jesus and want to be forgiven, they can be. If they have committed "marital adultery" against a mate by divorcing them to marry someone else or have been divorced and remarried because of

fornication and then find out that they have done wrong, they need to repent and turn to Jesus like everybody else. They do not have to destroy their established families and leave their children without one parent in the home to do it. **There is no example anywhere in the New Testament of that being required. Not one example. Not even a word. No not one. There is not even a hint that repentance demands breaking up an established family. They definitely should not divorce the one they have married because that would be doing the very thing they should have repented of. One does not repent of an unauthorized divorce by doing the same thing again.** Repentance demands a change in attitude which results in a change in action and direction. A person who repents of divorcing (or being divorced because of sin) does not divorce to prove they have repented of divorcing. When David, who had married Bathsheba, repented of the sin of adultery, he also repented of taking Uriah's wife to be his wife (2 Sam. 12:9). He determined not to do the same thing again (Ps. 51). But he did not divorce her! If a person has committed marital adultery against a mate in the past, it seems rather strange to teach them that they must commit marital adultery against their present mate in order to correct it. Those who demand that a person repent of divorcing by divorcing again need to carefully consider David and his repentance and what that involved. In fact, they might even "profit" from some of their own sins, mistakes, and misunderstandings!

24

WHAT ABOUT DESERTION AND THE RIGHT TO REMARRY?

1. I believe that in Matthew 19:3-9, Jesus was dealing with what the Pharisees taught about "putting away" or divorcing a mate in order to marry another, while in 1 Corinthians 7:15 the Holy Spirit deals with "desertion." There is an obvious difference in wanting to "put away" a mate in order to marry someone else and in being "deserted" by an unbelieving mate. 1 Corinthians 7:15 reads, *"But if the unbeliever departs, let him depart; a brother or a sister is not under bondage in such cases. But God has called us to peace."*

2. If the deserted believer cannot remarry, then they are definitely still "under bondage" of some kind! According to some the verse should read: "But if the unbelieving depart let him depart the brother or sister is 'still under bondage' in such cases." It cannot be both ways. They are either "not under bondage" as it pertains to marriage or they are "still under bondage" as it pertains to marriage.

3. If "not under bondage" means only that they are not bound to stay with their unbelieving mate who leaves, then that would be needless for Paul to say. It would be impossible for one to be a companion to—"stay with"—one who had "departed."

4. In verse 11, Paul spoke to those Christians who were married at the time and said if a Christian departs from a Christian they should "remain unmarried" or be "reconciled", which would be the ideal thing to do if both wanted to be faithful to the Lord's teaching. But if he meant that the believer here in verse 15 had to "remain unmarried," why did he not say it? The fact that he said the deserted believer is "not under bondage" indicates that they are not bound to remain single or be reconciled to someone who has deserted them, as was the case with those he referred to in verse 11.

5. The only "bondage" discussed in 1 Corinthians 7:1-15 is the "marriage bond." This is easily seen by just reading the verses. For example:

> In verse 2, Paul says "let each man have his own wife and let each woman have her own husband." This is a reference to being "bound" in marriage.
>
> In verses 3-6, he is speaking about the sexual privilege of those who are "bound" in marriage.
>
> In verse 7, he says it is a "gift" to be celibate and not "bound" in a marriage.

In verse 8, he says that it is good not to be "bound" in marriage.

In verse 9, he says it is better to be "bound" in marriage than to burn with passion.

In verses 10 and 11, he speaks to two believers who are "bound" in marriage.

In verses 11-14, he is speaking to believers who are "bound" in marriage to unbelievers.

6. In verse 15, he is still speaking to believers who are "bound" in marriage to unbelievers and says "if the unbelieving depart." Depart from what? In light of the entire context, it must be the marriage bond. In other words, if the unbeliever breaks the "marriage covenant" which "bound" the unbeliever to him/her, then the believer is no longer bound to the unbeliever who has "deserted" him/her.

7. **If the deserted believer is "not under bondage," then it seems to me that the deserted believer in this verse is "free" or "loosed" from the marriage bond and is as though they had never been married in the first place.** If a deserted believer is "not under bondage," and therefore free from the marriage bond, then that means that he/she is not still married to his/her ex-wife/husband in any sense. They are not married in man's sight. They are not married in God's sight. And they are not married in anybody's sight that can see! If they are "loosed" from the marriage bond or not bound by the marriage bond then they are "free" from the marriage that bound them and are in an "unmarried" state.

8. The question then is: Can an "unmarried" person who is "loosed" from the marriage bond remarry without sinning? Read the answer from the Bible for yourself in the very chapter where he said that the believer is "not under bondage" if deserted (1 Cor. 7:15). Just a few verses later, he authorized the right of marriage to those "loosed from" a mate, which would include, but not be limited to, the deserted believer. Read it for yourself in 1 Corinthians 7:27-28.

> *Are you bound to a wife? Do not seek to be loosed.* **Are you loosed from a wife?** *Do not seek a wife. But even **if you do marry, you have not sinned**; and if a virgin marries, she has not sinned. Nevertheless such will have trouble in the flesh, but I would spare you.*

9. Notice carefully that the Bible clearly says if you have been "loosed," or "released" (divorced), and are unmarried, then "if you do marry, you have not sinned." Why is that the case with the deserted believer? Because of the fact that the marriage to his/her first husband/wife is as though it had never happened.

10. This is the view that I read from Foy Wallace, Jr. and R. L. Whiteside when I first started preaching and the one that I have believed for most of my preaching career which, as of this writing, is over forty years. **And this is also the view I understood when I first read the passage and the view which the majority would understand by simply reading the verse. We actually must have some help to misunderstand it!**

11. Special note: One popular objection to this view is that the word translated "bondage" is not the word used for the "marriage" bond. To that I would say the following:

> As far I know, there is no Greek or English word that means "marriage bond."

> The context, not the Greek word, must determine what "bondage" is being referred to. We have already proven that the marriage bond is the only "bond" referred to in the context.

> The "bondage" that a believer is in if the unbeliever stays is the same bondage that the believer is "not under" if the unbeliever leaves. If the unbeliever stays, the believer is "bound" in marriage to the unbeliever; so if the unbeliever leaves, the believer is not under the marriage bond with the unbeliever. How much simpler could it be than that?

12. Furthermore, anything that I have to know the Greek to understand, I personally do not believe. I do not know any "Greek" and have trouble understanding it when someone tries to teach it to me. Personally, I have no interest in learning the Greek or Hebrew languages. If I studied either of them the rest of my life, I would most likely not know any more than those who translated our standard translations of the Bible. Other ships (believers) may venture more...but this little boat (preacher) will stay on the shore. Therefore, I must be able to understand the truth from standard translations of the Bible in order for me to believe it or teach it.

I also believe that the Bible itself is its own best interpreter. I believe that most people can understand what the Bible teaches on all important subjects just by studying the Bible in any standard translation without knowing anything about the original languages.

13. Whether a mate is *deceased* or *released*, the marriage on earth has *ceased*. We are not bound to one who is *dead* and we cannot be bound to one who has *departed*.

14. One final point is that some who teach that the "bondage" does not refer to the "marriage" bond believe that Paul is saying that a believer is not a "slave" to the unbeliever but is still somehow tied to the marriage. However, the reason a mate is "not under bondage" to a "deserter" is because God has called us to "peace." But there is no peace in having to stay in a marriage relationship with one who has abandoned the marriage covenant. What exactly is the difference between not being a slave to stay with a person, but being a slave who has to stay married to the person in some sense? What is the difference in being a slave to the marriage but not a slave to the person? If I am a slave to the marriage then I am a slave to the person in the marriage. If not, why not? Furthermore, I am most certainly a "slave" to the marriage and the person if I cannot dissolve the marriage with a person who has abandoned the covenant.

Note: For more on this point see Appendix number six: WHAT HAVE OTHERS SAID ABOUT DESERTION AND THE RIGHT TO REMARRY?

25

WHAT IF A BELIEVER
DESERTS A BELIEVER?

1. Someone may wonder, "Does 1 Corinthians 7:15 apply to a believer who is deserted by a *believing* partner?" My answer is yes, for a number of reasons. The principle is the same: a person cannot stay in a marriage covenant with one who has made up their mind to leave it for good.

2. The ideal thing for two believers who separate or divorce is to "remain unmarried" or "be reconciled," which is what Paul taught in this very chapter in verses 10 and 11. As long as both remain faithful to the Lord's teaching on this subject, this is always best and the way it is supposed to work.

3. But if one of the marriage partners decides to make the separation or divorce permanent (by marrying someone else, or dating someone else, or refusing to consider reconciliation given enough time) and the deserted partner knows in their own heart that there is no hope of reconciliation, then I believe they are totally free, as though the marriage never existed in the first place. And since the "deserted" believer is

"unmarried," Paul said the "unmarried" do not sin by getting married (1 Cor. 7:27-28).

4. It is also important to understand that a believer can become an "unbeliever." In Hebrews 3:1, the writer addresses "holy brethren" who were "partakers of the heavenly calling." Just a few verses later, in Hebrews 3:12, he writes, *"Beware, brethren, lest there be in any of you an evil heart of **unbelief** in departing from the living God…"*

5. When a believer develops an "unbelieving heart" then he/she becomes an "unbeliever." If that happens (which is most likely the case in many, if not most, of the cases of marriage desertion), then we have an "unbeliever" who "deserts" the marriage covenant, and the believer who is "deserted" is clearly "not under bondage" in such cases (1 Cor. 7:15).

6. It is true that in 1 Corinthians 7:12-15 Paul was answering a specific question that they had asked about a believer being married to an unbeliever. But the principle he taught about "desertion" would apply to all cases of "abandonment."

7. For example, what Jesus taught in Matthew 19:1-11 about divorce for fornication was primarily applied to two believers, according to Paul's statement in 1 Corinthians 7:10-11. But the principle would also apply to any and all marriages. If an "unbeliever" divorces his "unbelieving" mate in order to marry someone else, then they too "commit adultery" against their mate by divorcing them (Mk 10:11). In the same way, a "believer," who "deserts" the marriage covenant that he has with another "believer," is guilty of "desertion" and leaves the one who is "deserted" free from the marriage bond.

8. Paul clearly teaches in 1 Corinthians 7:15 that one who has been "deserted" is "not under bondage."

9. Suppose, for example, that the Corinthians had asked Paul, "What is a believer who is married to an unbeliever to do if the unbeliever dies?" We all know that they would be told that, in that case, the believer would no longer be bound by the marriage covenant made with the unbeliever. We would also understand that the "principle involved" would also apply to a believer married to a believer who died.

10. It does not matter who "deserts" a marriage covenant (believer or unbeliever); it is impossible to be bound to or stay in a "marriage covenant" with one who has "departed" for good.

11. The teaching of the Lord in 1 Corinthians 7 on marriage is the ideal way to deal with marital issues confronting believers. Note:

> Ideally, for two married believers: no separation or divorce. *"A wife is not to depart from her husband...And a husband is not to divorce his wife"* (1 Cor. 7:10).

> If that does not work and there is a separation, then God regulates the next step. Both need to *"remain unmarried or be reconciled"* (1 Cor. 7:11).

> If that does not work and one of the "believers" marries someone else, starts dating someone

else, or does something else that indicates they are unwilling to "remain unmarried" or "be reconciled," then God regulates the next step in principle (using a believer who is deserted by an unbeliever) by teaching that "desertion" leaves one "not under bondage" to the marriage covenant.

Since a deserted believer is "unmarried" or "loosed" from a deserting partner (whether "deserted" by an unbeliever who rejects Christ altogether, or by a believer who refuses to respect the Lord's teaching in this matter), then if the deserted believer marries someone else "they have not sinned" (1 Cor. 7:27-28).

26

WHAT ABOUT REFUSING TO BAPTIZE THOSE WHO HAVE BEEN DIVORCED AND REMARRIED?

1. The Bible is very clear about what to do with those who have been divorced and are now remarried. God could not have chosen a place any better than the church in Corinth to teach us what to do about those who have made marriage mistakes (or messes) and now want to come to Jesus for forgiveness. They can be forgiven and they do not have to divorce their mates, destroy their families, and leave their children without one parent in the home to do it.

2. Corinth was one of the most sinful cities in the New Testament. The church was composed of some who had been wicked in numerous ways. Paul's reference to their former conduct makes that very plain. Observe the list:

> *Do you not know that the unrighteous will not inherit the kingdom of God? Do not be*

deceived. Neither fornicators, nor idolaters, nor adulterers, nor homosexuals, nor sodomites, nor thieves, nor covetous, nor drunkards, nor revilers, nor extortioners will inherit the kingdom of God. And such were some of you. But you were washed, but you were sanctified, but you were justified in the name of the Lord Jesus and by the Spirit of our God. (1 Cor. 6:9-11).

3. This was a partial list of the type of sinners who were converted in Corinth. Included in the list were fornicators and adulterers. **For anyone to think that there were not numerous MDR couples in the Corinthian church is both naïve and foolish. Surely there were many who had divorced and remarried before they heard the gospel and were baptized into Christ.** Did they sin in doing so? I'm sure that some did.

4. What course of action does God require in those cases? We are not left to wonder. God answered that question in the very next chapter of this book. In doing so, three times he said to "remain in the calling/state" that they were in when they were converted. Read it for yourself:

> *But as God has distributed to each one, **as the Lord has called** each one, **so let him walk.** And so I ordain **in all the churches.*** (1 Cor. 7:17).

> *Let each one **remain in the same calling** in which he was called. (1 Cor. 7:20).*

> *Brethren, let each one* **remain with God in that**
> **state** *in which he was called.* (1 Cor. 7:24).

5. Three times Paul said to "remain in the calling" they were in when they were baptized. This was the rule "in all the churches," not just in Corinth. But does it include marriage relationships? The answer to this question is also in this context. Read it for yourself:

"Are you **bound** *to a wife?* **Do not seek to be loosed.** *Are you loosed from a wife? Do not seek a wife"* (1 Cor. 7:27).

6. Observe carefully the application Paul makes. Those "bound to a wife" are told, "Do not seek to be loosed." That is, do not seek a divorce. Why would he say that? It was because that was the "calling" or "state" that they were in when they became Christians. Married couples are told to stay married. He did not say, "Are you bound to your *first* wife?," but, "Are you bound to *a* wife?"

7. Many of those in the Corinthian church had no doubt committed marital adultery in the past against a marriage partner, and had since remarried. What could they do about it now? Nothing! One cannot change what has happened in the past in these cases. God knows it and we know it.

8. There must have been many, many, many MDR cases among the Jews and Gentiles. Yet nothing is said about what to do about it, except turn to Jesus for forgiveness. And three times in one chapter, he said "abide in the calling/state" in which one is "called" (1 Cor. 7:17, 20, 24). It is in this context

that he said, *"Are you bound to a wife, seek not to be loosed"* (1 Cor. 7:27).

9. In commenting on this point Foy Wallace, Jr. had this to say:

It is in this connection that the apostle added in verse 20, "Let every man abide in the same calling wherein he was called," and it should serve as a check to some marriage-counseling preachers who are so readily disposed to break up marriage relationships that are not in conformity with their own imma-ture human opinions. (The Sermon on the Mount and the Civil State, pg.45).

10. There are already enough divorces in America without our preachers/leaders demanding more. Brethren need to realize that breaking up established families, leaving chil-dren without one parent in the home, refusing to baptize/fel-lowship MDR people and "demanding" that they "divorce" a faithful mate is serious, serious, serious business. I may be wrong about what I believe, but I had much rather err by being too merciful and letting the ones involved decide what they must do based on all of the evidence, than by being judg-mental and *deciding for them* on such a sensitive and serious issue. This is especially true considering all of the compli-cated marriage messes that people can get into. The very fact that some of the most dedicated/godly men (and best minds) among us have been woefully divided on the issue should serve as a warning to those who would destroy established families to proceed with caution. *To be honest, demanding divorce of those who want to come to Jesus sounds too much like the Pharisees for me!*

11. Of course, the basic problem in most cases usually goes back to the ridiculous idea that those "divorced" are "still married." If people realized that the "invisible clamp" or "mysterious mystical marriage magnet" or the "Catholic covenant" of marriage that supposedly holds a couple together that are divorced does not exist, then many of the marriage misunderstandings would be cleared up. When a couple is formally divorced, then that means they are not still married to each other in any sense or in anybody's sight. That is why it is called "divorce." **Divorce is the termination of a marriage—not an imaginary invisible continuation of the marriage that has ended.**

12. A lot of people in the world have committed adultery against a faithful mate by divorcing them to marry someone else and they need to repent of that sin. They need to decide not to divorce a faithful mate again. But they do not "keep on" committing adultery against a mate that they no longer have. There is not a standard translation of the Bible that I have read that says one "keeps on" committing adultery against the one from whom he/she is divorced.

13. It is interesting that when Hugo McCord translated 1 John 1:7 it was, "the blood of Jesus his Son *keeps on* cleansing us from every sin." But in none of the passages dealing with divorce did he translate it "keeps on" committing adultery. (*The Everlasting Gospel*). Remember that one cannot "keep on" committing adultery "against" a mate that does not exist or that he does not have.

14. By the way, those who refuse to fellowship those involved in MDR are just as wrong as those who refuse to baptize

them. They are simply waiting a little longer to judge them condemned. In a real sense, there is not any real difference in the views. Both are wrong.

27

ARE WE ENCOURAGING PEOPLE TO DIVORCE?

1. Does emphasizing what the Bible teaches about grace and forgiveness with regard to MDR encourage people to divorce? It could in some cases. Anytime you teach the truth on forgiveness for any sin and how grace applies to the sin, some might take advantage of it. Some evidently did that in the New Testament. They turned the "grace" of the Savior into a "license" to sin.

> For certain men have crept in unnoticed, who long ago were marked out for this condemnation, ungodly men, **who turn the grace of our God into lewdness** and deny the only Lord God and our Lord Jesus Christ (Jude 4).

2. Since there were "ungodly men" who "pervert the grace of our God into a license for immorality" (NIV), I would not be surprised if some do the same thing when they learn what the Bible actually teaches about MDR.

3. When we preach about how God will freely forgive the sin of fornication, it may be used by some as an excuse to commit the sin of fornication. The same could be true of lying, cheating, stealing, murder, and any number of other sins.

4. The thing I wonder about is why is divorce about the only sin that we make this argument about? Why has divorce almost become the "unpardonable" sin?

5. If I teach that young girls who have gotten pregnant and have children out of wedlock can be freely forgiven, and go on from where they are with the baby, am I "encouraging" them to have children outside of marriage? Absolutely not! *I am not encouraging them to do it...I am teaching that they can live through it!* If I teach a young girl who has had an abortion that she can be forgiven, am I encouraging people to have abortions? Absolutely not! *I am not encouraging them to do it...I am teaching that they can live through it.* If I teach young boys that have committed fornication or been involved in drunkenness that they can be forgiven of those sins, am I encouraging them to commit those sins? *Absolutely not! I am not encouraging them to do it...I am teaching that they can live through it!*

6. And what about the other side of the story? I might ask, "Does teaching people that they must stay in abusive marriages no matter what (unless their mate commits fornication) encourage mistreatment of spouses with their teaching?" I know personally of cases where this has happened. Are those preachers who teach what they believe about how marriages cannot be ended for any reason other than fornication or death responsible for the mistreatment?

7. The truth is that there are always some who will use *pardon* for *permission*. There are always some who will use *forgiveness of* sin as *freedom to* sin. But that does not make it wrong to teach the truth on any subject.

8. **In my judgment the good that teaching the truth on MDR will do for those involved far outweighs the fear of some who will use these truths as freedom to sin.** In other words, the liberty for MDR couples is more important to me than worrying about some using it as license. The freedom from guilt that Jesus offers far outweighs the fear of some misusing these facts.

28

What Do I Say to Those Who Have Been Divorced and Remarried?

1. I encourage them to seriously consider the conclusions in this book before they give up on the church. As stated in the beginning, divorce is sometimes an option and, sadly, in some cases it is the *only* option. **God Himself divorced Israel (Jer. 3:8).** I do not believe that we can divorce our faithful mates for just any and every cause. But on the other hand, we are not required to remain in abusive marriages, or remain in a marriage that causes us to be unfaithful to Jesus, or other reasons we have discussed in this book. There is no reason for breaking up your family because some preacher or elder does not approve of your marriage.

2. As I thought about how to end this book a lot of ideas came to mind. What do I say to those who have been hurt in a marital relationship or have hurt others, but have now come to Jesus and His church for help and healing? What do I say to those who are burdened with grief or guilt or both? What do

I want to leave them thinking about and focusing on? Here are my final thoughts to those involved in MDR!

3. I do admire and respect you for coming to Jesus for forgiveness and strength. Even though some of you knew the negative atmosphere that you would be in with some in the church you came anyway. Many of you were unjustly put away by a mate who simply wanted someone else. Some of you were abused both physically and emotionally. Some of you were deserted. Some of you were in marriages that did not work out for whatever reason. Some of you were put away because of your own unfaithfulness to a marriage partner. Some of you were guilty of abusing a faithful partner. Some of you were divorced for other reasons. Many of you have remarried and started over and most importantly turned to Jesus and the church for help and healing. I am sorry to say that in most cases, MDR people do not turn to Jesus, but you did. I am proud of you for making that decision. I encourage you to rest your hope fully on the grace and mercy of Jesus and go on from where you are now (Phil. 3:13-14; 1 Pet. 1:13).

4. Learn from the past but do not live in it. It may be OK to *glance* back, but do not *gaze* back. Whether your divorce was lawful or unlawful the results are the same and the previous marriage is over. If you are now in a new marriage relationship then learn from the mistakes and/or mistreatment of the past and help others involved in MDR do the same. In the church we can accept without approving. We can forgive without reproving. We can all focus on improving.

5. Those of us who have never been involved in MDR cannot relate to those who have been involved in MDR like you can.

I encourage you to use what you have learned to help others. If we read Psalms 51 which records David's prayer for forgiveness for adultery and murder, one of the things that you will learn is that when forgiven, he intended to *"teach transgressors Your ways And sinners shall be converted to You"* (Ps. 51:12-13). **I encourage you to use what has happened in your own lives to help others recover and discover the salvation and strength that Jesus gives us all.** Let others know that the gospel is good news for all—who come *"Just as I am"...married, divorced and remarried!*

29

WHAT ARE SOME THINGS FOR ALL OF US TO REMEMBER?

1. Marriage is a covenant between two people with God as a witness (Mal. 2:14). Ideally it is a permanent relationship that needs to be maintained in good times and bad. God's original/ideal plan is one man for one woman for life and that has never changed. See Matthew 19:4-6.

2. The view that marriage is non-dissolvable most likely came from the "Catholic Covenant" of marriage. God has never taught that a marriage cannot be dissolved by those involved. A formal divorce changes the course. It is the end of the marriage. There is no invisible clamp or mysterious mystical marriage magnet that holds a couple together that are divorced whether the divorce is lawful (authorized) or unlawful (unauthorized). The idea that marriage is non-dissolvable is not taught anywhere in the Bible and never has been. See Matthew 19:6.

3. God does authorize/sanction/approve divorce in some cases. All marital adultery involves covenant breaking but

not all breaking of the covenant involves marital adultery. (All murder involves killing but not all killing is murder.) If a person is authorized (given the right) to divorce a mate they must break the covenant in order to do so but it is not marital adultery. Marital adultery involves *unlawfully divorcing a faithful mate* especially in order to marry someone else or causing a divorce in order to marry. See Matthew 5:31-32.

4. It is always wrong to divorce a faithful mate in order to marry someone else, but it not wrong for a person who is already divorced to marry. See Matthew 19:9 and 1 Corinthians 7:27-28. In Matthew 19:9 and Matthew 5:31-32 Jesus is only dealing with one aspect of the marriage issue. He is only dealing with *divorcing* a faithful mate in order to marry someone else or *causing a divorce* in order to marry. This is not nearly the sum total of the marriage message.

5. **A person does not commit adultery by having sex with his/her spouse. The marriage relationship is an honorable state to be in even though the circumstances that brought it about may have been undesirable or even sinful.** See Hebrews 13:4. There is no Bible example of a person being guilty of committing adultery with one to whom he/she is legitimately married. The Samaritan woman had had five husbands which indicate that Jesus recognized that she had been in five legitimate marital relationships but was sinning by simply living with a man who was not her husband. See John 4:7-18.

6. The word "adultery" in the Bible always refers to covenant breaking in some sense. Marital adultery in the sense that Jesus used it in regard to marriage is the unlawful breaking

of the marriage covenant in order to marry someone else or causing a divorce in order to marry. There is no standard translation that I have read that teaches that one "keeps on committing adultery" with one to whom he/she is married. We all believe that we "commit adultery" against our mates if we divorce them in order to marry someone else because that is exactly what Jesus clearly says. See Mark 10:10-11. What I do not believe is that one "keeps on" committing adultery with one they are married to. The view that a divorced person who remarries "keeps on" committing adultery with one they are married to came about long after Jesus said what He did about it. See Matthew 19:9.

7. A marriage partner who has been divorced because of sexual immorality is released from the marriage bond and is no longer bound to the marriage nor is he/she bound to stay single. All of those "loosed" or divorced from a mate are allowed to marry whether the divorce was lawful or unlawful. See 1 Corinthians 7:27-28.

8. If a marriage partner deserts the marriage covenant a believer is not under bondage to that marriage regardless of what others may say. See 1 Corinthians 7:15. And they are free to remarry since they are "loosed" (divorced) from a mate. See 1 Corinthians 7:27-28. If a mate is unjustly put away they are in the same position as those who are deserted in the sense that neither of them are at fault. Both are allowed to remarry. See 1 Corinthians 7:27-28.

9. God did not require slaves to stay in a marriage where they were abused and neither does He require it of married people today. No marriage is ideal in all aspects and it

takes commitment to make marriage work, but neither is it designed to be an abusive ordeal. See Exodus 21:10-11; 1 Corinthians 7:12ff; and 2 Corinthians 6:14-17.

10. There is no example of refusing to baptize those involved in MDR. When writing to those in Corinth, which was one of the wickedest cities of the time, Paul told them three times to remain in the relationship that they were in when they became Christians which included marital relationships. This is the rule for all churches. See 1 Corinthians 7:17-28. Refusing to fellowship those who are MDR is the same as refusing to baptize them. This is simply delaying the unjust condemnation for a short time. (If I were not going to fellowship them as faithful Christians, neither would I baptize them.) **The view that we can baptize them but then not recognize them as faithful Christians after we do it makes no sense to me. In fact, it seems rather cruel and heartless!**

11. There is no example or command to break up an established family in order for one to become a Christian. One does not repent of a sin by committing the same sin again. (We do not repent of murdering someone in the past by murdering someone else in the present.) One does not repent of divorcing a former faithful mate by divorcing his/her present faithful mate. The Bible nowhere commands or commends any such thing! Those who demand that an MDR person divorce a faithful mate are commanding them to do the very thing that God hates. It is treacherous. It is condemned in no uncertain terms in both the Old and New Testaments. See Malachi 2:10-16 and Matthew 19:1-9.

12. Christians have often practiced unjust discrimination because of a misunderstanding of what they thought the Bible taught. We have all most likely been guilty of this practice at some point. Prejudice is hard to overcome whether it involves race or relationships. Giving up long held convictions is extremely hard no matter what the subject matter is. But honesty and faithfulness to the Lord and His word demand that we give up positions that are proven false regardless of how long we have held them or who it may offend.

13. God joins a couple when they meet His qualifications for marriage. These qualifications are that they be male and female and that they be joined to each other by covenant or agreement with God as a witness. Those who seek to associate MDR couples with same sex "marriages" or just "living together" without being married are seeking to compare a relationship that has always been legitimate with relationships that have never been legitimate. This kind of "reasoning?" is one reason I wrote this book. **Those who seek to compare a legitimately married couple to those who simply live together without marriage or to same sex "marriages" are obviously displaying what they really believe about MDR couples and are sometimes trying to prejudice people accordingly**.

14. The Pharisees controlled the religious thinking of the people when Jesus arrived on the scene. When He challenged their teaching, traditions and views they attacked His character, His motives and His message. He was lied about, falsely accused and castigated by those who wanted to control the Jewish nation. They were a *violent minority* who wanted to control the *silent majority*. The same thing

can happen among God's people today. Those who would seek to "control" believers today (some call it "policing the brotherhood") may use some of the same tactics. If so, so be it! Because the sanctity of marriage and the evils of unauthorized divorce demand that we stand for what we believe. **Established families are too important to our society to allow them to be destroyed because of the unfounded opinions of others who demand that MDR people divorce their present faithful mates and leave their children with only one parent in the home. Furthermore the souls of those involved in MDR are too valuable and their children are too precious for us to be intimidated by those who may want to dominate and/or manipulate our beliefs on these matters.**

15. The Pharisees were the ones who would "bind heavy burdens, hard to bear" on others but would not deal with their own hypocrisy, self-righteousness or sinfulness. See Matthew 23:4. In contrast to that, I believe that many leaders who demand divorce and/or breaking up established families whose marital status does not measure up to their views may (unlike the Pharisees) sincerely believe that what they teach is the truth. Their problem may involve a lack of comprehension and not necessarily a lack of compassion. However the negative results on MDR couples and their families are the same whether they are compassionate (?) or not.

16. According to some leaders a young lady and young man can live together without marriage for years and years and then break up and either of them can later get married, have children, and become Christians. But if they happen to get married and live together for *three weeks* and she finds out

that he is evil and abusive and she divorces him, then later remarries and has children, she must then divorce her present faithful mate and leave her children without one parent in the home in order be a Christian. Surely we can see that there is something seriously wrong with that message.

17. In some churches we can forgive fornicators, prostitutes, drunkards, child molesters, sex offenders, murderers, thieves, liars, adulterers, drug addicts, drug dealers and such like. They can repent and turn to Jesus and go on with their lives with their wives/husbands and children....unless, unless, unless they have made a marriage mistake themselves or married the wrong person in the past. In that case, they cannot go on with their wives/husbands and children. In those cases, according to some (and their numbers are steadily shrinking), they must divorce their mates and live single for the rest of their lives *even if they were deserted and/or physically abused and/or unjustly divorced by a marriage partner in the past*. If anyone actually thinks that that teaching sounds like the Jesus we read about in the Bible, then they do not know the Jesus I know and quite obviously don't know what the Bible teaches on this subject...in my judgment.

18. If you are divorced it is not a sin to marry. Whether you have been sinned against by an unfaithful mate (sexual immorality, desertion, abuse, etc.) or whether you have sinned against marriage yourself by your own unfaithfulness in the past, the results are the same. If you are "loosed" (divorced) from a mate, you do not sin by getting married. See 1 Corinthians 7:27-28.

19. Remember this above all. If you are married God wants to stay married. He told those who were married in Corinth to stay married. See 1 Corinthians 7:10-11. If you are bound (married) to a mate do not seek to be divorced. See 1 Corinthians 7:27. In other words, *"Therefore what God has joined together, let not man separate."* See Matthew 19:6.

Wayne Dunaway
November, 2014

APPENDIX 1

WHAT IS WRONG WITH TEACHING THAT THE MARRIAGE IS CONSUMMATED BY THE "SEXUAL UNION"?

1. If a couple is married as far as God is concerned at the point when the "sexual union" occurs, then they are not "married" at all in the eyes of God until that happens. If that is the case, there are some serious problems.

2. Do we preachers explain this to those we perform the ceremony for in all cases? Do they know that they have not reached the point where the marriage takes place when we pronounce them "husband and wife" and that the marriage relationship does not really exist in the eyes of God until it has been consummated? Do they understand that they must have sex for it to become a real "marriage" or "one flesh" relationship? Wouldn't they need to know up front that they only become "one flesh" with God's approval after (or is it during) the sexual union?

3. What about the people in the audience at a marriage ceremony who are listening? Would they not need to know that the exchanging of the vows is not actually a "marriage," but this only gives this couple the legal and moral right to cohabit? It seems to me that Christian preachers (and others who perform marriage ceremonies) would have the moral

obligation to tell all of those involved that God does not really consider this exchanging of the vows a marriage, but it is only the legalities of the state that we are accomplishing now. We could easily include this explanation in a marriage ceremony if it were really true.

4. If the couple have not reached the point that the marriage actually takes place in the sense that God considers them married when we pronounce them "husband and wife," but this is only a "marriage" in the sense that the legalities of the state are met and it is the intent of the couple to marry, and they only have the legal and moral right to cohabit, and are not actually married as far as God is concerned, then it seems to me that we have two "unmarried" people taking their clothes off, lusting after each other, fondling each other, and getting into bed with each other who are not really "one flesh" (or married). Where does God give the legalities of the state the power to make it legal and moral to "cohabit"? Hebrews 13:4 says that "marriage" is honorable and the marriage bed is undefiled, but if they are only married by the laws of the state but not the law of God, then the "bed" is filled with fornicators or adulterers. It is not "consummation," it is "fornication" regardless of how we try to explain it.

5. According to the Bible, a couple is married "by covenant" (agreement) with God as a "witness" (Mal. 2:14). Therefore, when I perform a "marriage ceremony" for a couple with God as a witness, I know exactly when and at what "point" they are actually and legitimately married. They are not actually married at the "beginning" of the ceremony. They are not yet married during the "middle" of the ceremony. But it is at the "end," after they both vowed/promised themselves to each other, that they are "married." It is at that "point"—when I pronounce them "husband and wife"—that they are married, totally and completely. If for some reason they cannot complete the ceremony (one of them gets sick or passes out, which has happened), then they are not married at all without completing the "marriage covenant" or ceremony. The only plausible alternative to this view would be the one that says they are actually married in the eyes of God when they agree and make a covenant with each other privately. In other words, it may be possible for some to argue that they are married in God's sight before

the ceremony, but there is no way that they are still unmarried in any sense after the ceremony.

6. According to those who hold the "sexual experience" idea of marriage, the couple becomes one flesh when, with God's blessing, they join in sexual union. My question is: At what "point" during this "sexual union" do they become one flesh in "God's sight"? Is it at the "beginning" of the intercourse? (If so, then they are married without having to complete the sexual union.) If it is at the "end" of the intercourse, what if they did not get finished (because of pain or other problems that can and have happened), are they married anyway? What if only one of them "climaxes" but the other did not? Is it still a marriage? What if they tried to have sex but could not (virginity/size, etc.)? Are they married anyway? (One couple told me that it took "weeks" and medical help before they could have intercourse. Were they married during this waiting period or not?) I know this may sound silly to some, but if the "not married until they have sex" idea of marriage is true; these are very important and even crucial questions. It would be important to know the "point" that I became *actually* married in God's sight and with God's blessing. But actually these questions are silly because the view of marriage that says we are not married until we have sex is silly. It shows how utterly ridiculous this whole sexual union idea of becoming "one flesh" or "consummating" the marriage really is.

7. I do not believe that there is any such thing as being "partly" married, or "somewhat" married, or married in "one sense," but not in another "sense." (In my judgment that is absolute *nonsense*.) We are either married or we are not married. If we "get married" in the ceremony, then we do not "get married" in the bed, but if we "get married" in the bed, then we do not "get married" in the ceremony.

8. Malachi gives us the Lord's definition of what is involved in being married. All married couples are married "by covenant" or by an agreement/vow/promise to be companions to each other for life. *"She is your companion and your wife by covenant"* (Mal. 2:14).

9. Where is the statement in the Bible that says we are married "by the sexual union"? Or where does the Bible say we are married "by being one flesh in the sexual union"?

10. God says a man is "one flesh" with his wife when he "leaves" father and mother and "cleaves" (KJV) or "holds fast" (ESV) to his wife. He does not say that he becomes one flesh by leaving his parents and having sex with his wife. Marriage is not a "sexual experience," it is a "covenant relationship."

11. There are those who say something like: It is God who joins husband and wife and makes them one flesh and the one flesh relationship involves sexual union (1 Corinthians 6:16). Therefore, it is those who become one flesh in the sexual union that God forbids putting asunder (Matthew 19:6).

12. This is an interesting and popular concept, but it puts far too much emphasis on sex and not enough emphasis on the commitment, which involves the promise/pledge/vow to be companions for life. Some say that a couple becomes "one flesh" with God's blessings only when they join together in "sexual union." This implies (intended or not) that the "sexual union" is more important than the vows or commitment that they make to each other. The "covenant" made with each other is only state legalities and some say it can be annulled at will by the couple involved. But once there is "sex" then God gets involved and puts an "imaginary clamp" on the whole process and marriage is real and consummated.

13. This view implies that marriage is really a "sexual experience" as much as or more so than a "covenant relationship." This is simply not true, and the consequences of such a false view are staggering.

14. The marriage should last long after the desire for sex has ended. If we teach and believe that the "commitment" does not make a couple "one flesh," but leave the impression (intended or not) that the "sex act" does, that is way too much for me. The "covenant" (commitment) that they make to each other is how God makes them "one flesh" and the

"covenant" (commitment) is how God keeps them "one flesh." But if I believed that the "sexual union" is how God made them "one flesh," then I would also believe that the "sexual union" is how God keeps them "one flesh." Which means that when the sexual union, by which God "makes" and "keeps" them "one flesh," is over (because of age, disability etc)…so is the marriage.

15. Another, perhaps far more serious, consequence of this view is that it would literally mean that a man could divorce his faithful wife and marry someone else as many times as he wanted to as long as he did not have sex with his new wife. Someone may object, "Who would marry someone and not have sex with her?" Think of an elderly man who for health reasons has no interest in sex, or perhaps cannot even have sex anymore, but he finds a woman whose company he prefers to that of his wife. (I personally know of cases where people who were very advanced in years divorced their mates because they did not like them anymore or did not want to be around them anymore). So this man divorces his present, faithful mate and marries someone else. This view would mean that he did exactly what Jesus said—divorced his mate and married someone else—but did not "commit adultery" in so doing because he did not have sex with his new wife. Jesus said that divorcing and remarrying someone else is "adultery." This man did that, but, according to the "sex is how people get married" idea, did not commit adultery. **Any view that makes what Jesus said wrong is a view that must be rejected outright.**

APPENDIX 2

IF "ONE FLESH" DOES NOT REFER TO THE SEX ACT, WHAT DOES FIRST CORINTHIANS 6:16-17 MEAN?

1. The verses read as follows:

> *Or do you not know that he who is joined to a harlot is one body with her? For "the two," He says, "shall become one flesh." But he who is joined to the Lord is one spirit with Him.*

2. It sounds like Paul is referring to the sex act here and calling it "one flesh." Is he? Or is he saying that one is "joined" to a harlot in "spirit" and that the mutual agreement (covenant) to have sex is expressed by the sex act.

3. Paul's point is that what is expressed by the "body" of the harlot and the man who has sex with her has already been mutually agreed on by the two involved. They are united (one flesh) in their minds and intentions in this decision, and this agreement is expressed in the physical relationship they have.

4. The emphasis in this context is on being "joined" to a harlot. One is joined to a harlot in mind first and foremost and this is only expressed by the body. This is Paul's point here and it harmonizes with God's teaching about becoming "one flesh" in the marriage relationship.

5. Note also Paul's application concerning the man being "one flesh" with the harlot. He contrasts being "one flesh" with that harlot with being one "in spirit" with the Lord. Therefore, it is clear that when he speaks of one being "joined to" or "one flesh" with the harlot, he is referring to what is going on in the minds that is simply expressed by the bodies. What is expressed by the body has already been agreed to in the spirit or mind. Just as a husband is joined to and is "one flesh" with his wife and he expresses it by the joining of bodies in sex, the man who decides to have sex with a harlot is "one flesh" (united) with her in that decision. This is the whole point of the "one flesh" statements. It is being united in a "covenant" or agreement to have sex that constitutes being "one flesh" with a harlot.

6. The contrast that I believe Paul is making is made simple in my paraphrase as follows.

> He who is joined to a harlot in spirit/mind/agreement becomes one with her and follows through by having sex. This is like the marriage covenant in a sense for the "two" shall become "one flesh." "But" (in contrast to being joined in spirit to a harlot) believers are one in spirit with the Lord."

7. Read the verses again with this point in mind.

> *Or do you not know that he who is **joined to a harlot** is one body with her? For "the two," He says, "shall become one flesh." But he who is **joined to the Lord** is one spirit with Him.*

8. Note that the contrast Paul is making is a contrast between "one who is joined to a harlot" (vs. 16) and one "who is joined to the Lord"

(vs. 17). The contrast is not about having sex, but a contrast between being one in spirit (one flesh) with the harlot in the decision to have sex, and being one spirit with the Lord in being united (one flesh, Eph. 5:31-32) with Him.

9. The meaning of the entire context is that the "commitment" to have sex with a harlot (become one body with her) is the same as the "commitment" to be married (be a companion to a wife) which is the same "commitment" believers have made to the Lord (be faithful to His word).

10. I realize that some may reject this view and say that I am reading into the text something that is not there. But consider this carefully: If what I have presented is not the meaning of 1 Corinthians 6:16-17, but Paul is teaching that we "become one flesh" with someone — even a prostitute — by having sex with her, then people are "one flesh" and *therefore married to everyone they have sex with*. No preacher or church leader I know teaches this. They know what the ramifications of such a ridiculous idea would be. But this is the logical conclusion to the idea that to be "one flesh" with someone is to "have sex" with someone. Is a man or woman married to everyone they have sex with? If you say no, then you should admit that what I contend could be the truth regarding Paul's statement and is a plausible meaning. What Paul taught here must harmonize with the other passages dealing with the "one flesh" statements and in my judgment it does.

APPENDIX 3

WHAT IS JESUS CORRECTING IN THE SERMON ON THE MOUNT?

1. We must understand that, in the Sermon on the Mount, when Jesus said things like, "you have heard that it was said" (Matt. 5:21, 27, 31, etc.), He was not talking about what "Moses" said and taught, but what the "Scribes and Pharisees" were saying and teaching. As the religious teachers of the day, they had misunderstood, misapplied, and misused most of the things that God had intended in the moral requirements of the Law of Moses. They had either changed God's commands altogether or misapplied what God had said in the commands. This is what Jesus was correcting in His teaching. The Law of Moses was "holy and just and good" in its moral precepts and commandments (Rom. 7:12). God did not "create" sin by giving the "law" through Moses. Sin already existed long before the Law of Moses was given.

2. We must keep in mind throughout the sermon that Jesus is both *explaining* and *exposing*. He is explaining what God actually meant in giving the moral requirements in the Law of Moses. And He was exposing what the Scribes and Pharisees were teaching about the Law. They had "made the commandment of God of no effect by their tradition" (Mt. 15:6). Jesus specifically told His disciples to "beware" of the teaching of the Pharisees (Mt. 16:12). They "justified themselves" (Lk. 16:15) and appeared righteous "outwardly," but inwardly were full of hypocrisy and deceit. (Matt. 23:28).

3. In the Sermon on the Mount, Jesus taught them what the Law of Moses actually meant and, at the same time, exposed the Scribes and Pharisees for changing, corrupting, and making void God's commandments by their false teaching. They were false teachers whom Jesus described as "wolves" in sheep's clothing (Mt. 7:15). In the sermon, notice how Jesus taught the same thing that Moses did on the following points.

4. *"You shall not murder"* (Mt. 5:21). Jesus explained that when God said not to murder He was not just talking about the "act" itself. He was also condemning the attitude of heart that leads to murder. He explained that the attitude that leads one to want to murder is the real problem and that we should seek to settle differences in the quickest and easiest way possible before it leads to all kind of problems—including wanting to murder someone else—and we bring judgment on ourselves. This same truth was taught in the overall teaching of the Old Testament. Jesus was not changing God's moral law on this subject.

The Law of Moses taught the same thing about anger that Jesus did, because it taught men to "do unto others as you would have them do to you" (Mt. 7:12). The Law taught men to *"Love your neighbor as yourself"* (Lev. 19:18; Mt. 22:39-40). The Old Testament warns against "anger" and taught men to be careful what they say and do when they are angry just as Jesus did here.

> **Cease from anger**, *and forsake wrath; do not fret—it only causes harm.* (Ps. 37:8).

> *A wrathful man stirs up strife, but he who is* **slow to anger** *allays contention.* (Prov. 15:18).

> *The discretion of a man makes him* **slow to anger**, *and his glory is to overlook a transgression.* (Prov. 19:11).

> *Do not hasten in your spirit to be* **angry**, *for* **anger** *rests in the bosom of fools.* (Ecc. 7:9).

Obviously the Jewish leaders did not teach this and they certainly did not practice it. They only thought or taught that it is wrong to commit the "act" of murder but did not teach people what the Old Testament taught about the attitude that leads to murder. In doing so, they could justify themselves (Lk. 16:15) because they were angry with Jesus and others for no reason.

5. *You have heard that it was said to those of old, 'You shall not commit adultery.' But I say to you that whoever looks at a woman to lust for her has already committed adultery with her in his heart.* (Matt. 5:27-28).

Jesus explained that when Moses gave this law, he was not just talking about the "act" itself, but also the lust in the heart that leads to committing the act. Moses himself taught that one should not "covet (desire/lust after) your neighbor's wife" (Ex. 20:17). Moses and others in the Old Testament clearly taught that it is wrong for a man to lust after a woman in his heart.

> *And you shall have the tassel, that you may look upon it and remember all the commandments of the* LORD *and do them, and that you may not follow the* **harlotry** *to which* **your own heart** *and* **your own eyes are inclined**, (Num. 15:39).*

> **Do not lust** *after her beauty* **in your heart**, *nor let her allure you with her eyelids.* (Prov. 6:25).

> *And there a woman met him, with the attire of a harlot, and a crafty heart…With her enticing speech she caused him to yield…Now therefore, listen to me, my children; Pay attention to the words of my mouth…Do not let* **your heart** *turn aside to her ways…*(Prov. 7:6-27).

> *Who may ascend into the hill of the* LORD*? Or who may stand in His holy place? He who has clean hands and a* **pure heart**… (Ps. 24:3-4).

The Pharisees were an "adulterous" generation (Mt. 16:4). They were full of "uncleanness" (Mt. 23:27). According to Strong's Concordance, the word "uncleanness" means: "in a moral sense: the impurity of lustful, luxurious, profligate living." When we look at the other ten times this word is used in the New Testament, it is obvious that it refers primarily to "sexual uncleanness." (See Rom. 1:24; 6:19; 2 Cor. 12:21; Eph. 4:19; 5:3, 5; Col. 3:5; 1 Thess. 2:3; 4:7; 2 Pet. 2:10). **Therefore, the Scribes and Pharisees were obviously lusting after women and sometimes putting their faithful wives away in order to marry them. In other cases, they were breaking up marriages in order to get the women they wanted. This is, no doubt, one of the reasons Jesus brought the subject up about committing adultery in the heart.** He was not only teaching that it is sin, but also condemning the Jewish leaders and others who were full of sexual uncleanness (Mt. 23:27).

6. This leads Jesus to expose what they were teaching about divorce.

> *"Furthermore it has been said, 'Whoever divorces his wife, let him give her a certificate of divorce.' But I say to you that whoever divorces his wife for any reason except sexual immorality causes her to commit adultery; and whoever marries a woman who is divorced commits adultery.* (Matt. 5:31).

This was a part of what Moses taught, but not in the sense that the Pharisees had interpreted it. They had conveniently left part of what Moses said completely out. Moses did not just say that a man could divorce his wife by simply giving her a "certificate of divorce" and sending her away. Moses said if he found some "uncleanness" in her, he could put her away. Jesus explained that the husband who put her away must do so because he has found some "sexual immorality" in her, which is exactly what Moses had taught. Otherwise, he causes it to appear that she has committed "uncleanness" or "sexual immorality." By putting her away he causes it to appear that she has "broken the marriage covenant" and is guilty of "uncleanness" (or marital adultery). See Deuteronomy 24:1-4.

As with the other subjects, the Pharisees were teaching that a man could put away his faithful wife for "any cause" as long as he gave her the "bill of divorcement." She did not have to be guilty of "uncleanness" like Moses actually said. They obviously taught that one does not sin by putting away his faithful wife in order to marry someone else, but Jesus said doing so "causes her" to "commit adultery," even if she is not guilty of doing anything wrong.

And whoever marries one who is "put away" because of "uncleanness" or "sexual immorality" is committing adultery because he is also responsible for breaking up the marriage covenant between a husband and wife. I believe that the reason Jesus said this is because the Pharisees, who were "adulterous" (Mt. 16:4) and full of (sexual) "uncleanness" (Mt. 23:27), were committing fornication with other men's wives and causing them to be put away, thus destroying the marriage covenant between that couple. And, of course, the same thing happens today. Anyone who causes the break up of a marriage is "committing adultery" (sinning) against the innocent marriage partner in that marriage that he helps breaks up.

7. *"Again you have heard that it was said to those of old, 'You shall not swear falsely, but shall perform your oaths to the Lord'* (Matt. 5:33). This is what Moses taught, but the Pharisees had corrupted what Moses taught to such an extent that they taught that it was right to lie and not even tell the truth at all. The Pharisees obviously taught that the only oaths that one had to perform were those made "to the Lord" and they were the ones who decided which oaths were made to the Lord and which were not. In other words, they decided which oaths were binding and which oaths were not. Jesus made this clear when He was condemning their hypocrisy in Matthew 23. Observe the reading:

*"Woe to you, blind guides, who say, 'Whoever swears by the temple, **it is nothing**; but whoever swears by the gold of the temple, **he is obliged to perform it**. Fools and blind! For which is greater, the gold or the temple that sanctifies the gold? And, 'Whoever swears by the altar, **it is nothing**; but whoever swears by the gift that is on it, **he is obliged to perform it.**' Fools and blind! For which is greater, the gift or the altar*

that sanctifies the gift? Therefore he, who swears by the altar, swears by it and by all things on it. He, who swears by the temple, swears by it and by Him who dwells in it. And he, who swears by heaven, swears by the throne of God and by Him who sits on it. (Mt. 23:16-22).

Observe that the Scribes and Pharisees taught that it was not a binding oath if one swears a certain way. In other words, one could swear by the temple that he was telling the truth and yet be lying and it would not be wrong to lie as long as he did not swear by the *gold* of the temple. This is the kind of ungodly teaching that Jesus was correcting in the Sermon on the Mount.

8. *"You have heard that it was said, 'An eye for an eye and a tooth for a tooth.' But I tell you not to resist an evil person. But whoever slaps you on your right cheek, turn the other to him also"* (Mt. 5:38-39). The Pharisees were obviously teaching that this command applies to personal vengeance. In other words, whatever someone does to hurt you, you can do the same to them. Jesus explained that Moses was not referring to personal vengeance when he wrote this command. God never taught personal vengeance against others.

When Moses said "eye for eye" he was referring to the right of the government to exercise vengeance on evildoers. It was and is God's way of executing wrath on murderers and the like. Observe what Moses actually said:

> *"One witness shall not rise against a man concerning any iniquity or any sin that he commits; by the mouth of **two or three witnesses** the matter shall be established. If a false witness rises against any man to testify against him of wrongdoing, then both men in the controversy shall stand before the LORD, before the priests and the **judges** who serve in those days. And the **judges** shall make careful inquiry, and indeed, if the witness is a false witness, who has testified falsely against his brother, then you shall do to him as he thought to have done to his brother; so you shall put away the evil from*

> *among you. And those who remain shall hear and fear,*
> *and hereafter they shall not again commit such evil*
> *among you. Your eye shall not pity: life shall be for*
> *life,* **eye for eye, tooth for tooth, hand for hand, foot**
> **for foot"** (Deuteronomy 19:15-21).

Observe that it was the judges who were to render the verdict for punishment for sins and this only after "careful inquiry" and on the testimony of "witnesses." This has nothing to do with God authorizing personal vengeance against another person.

The Law of Moses taught that if someone was breaking into a person's house, that person could kill him as a matter of personal protection. But one was not allowed to go out later and hunt him down and kill him as a matter of personal vengeance. Notice what Moses said:

> *If the thief is found breaking in, and he is struck so that*
> *he dies, there shall be no guilt for his bloodshed. If the*
> *sun has risen on him, there shall be guilt for his blood-*
> *shed.* (Exodus 22:2-3).

Observe that personal protection is allowed, while personal vengeance is denied. Jesus explained that God taught us to do good to others and not retaliate. As a matter of fact, Jesus Himself said that a man would not allow his house to be broken into (Matt. 24:43), but He, like Moses, also forbids taking personal vengeance (Matt. 5:39-42).

The Law and the prophets taught, *"do unto others as you would they do to you"* (Matt. 7:12) and to love your neighbor as "yourself' (Matt. 22:39-40). This is exactly what Jesus is explaining in the Sermon on the Mount. Jesus is emphasizing that God has always wanted us to "overcome evil with good."

The Old Testament taught the exact same thing as Jesus did in this sermon. God said, through Moses, *"Vengeance is mine and recompense"* (Deut. 32:35). Paul's application of this statement is in the New Testament in Romans 12:19-21 which reads as follows:

Beloved, do not avenge yourselves, but rather give place to wrath; for it is written, Vengeance is mine, I will repay," says the Lord. Therefore "If your enemy is hungry, feed him; if he is thirsty, give him a drink; for in so doing you will heap coals of fire on his head." Do not be overcome by evil, but overcome evil with good.

Observe that Paul told the saints in Rome not to "avenge yourselves." Why? Because of what God had "written" in the Old Testament in Deuteronomy 32:35 and reaffirmed by both Jesus in the Sermon on the Mount and Paul in Romans.

9. Consider also that Jesus said:

"You have heard that it was said, 'You shall love your neighbor and hate your enemy.' But I say to you, love your enemies, bless those who curse you, do good to those who hate you, and pray for those who spitefully use you and persecute you, (Matt. 5:43-44).

Moses did teach that we should love our neighbors, which the Pharisees were right about. But he did not teach that we are to "hate" our enemies. In fact, Moses taught what Jesus did. Like Jesus, He taught that men were to "do good to enemies." Observe what Moses wrote:

*If you meet your **enemies'** ox or his donkey going astray, you shall surely **bring it back to him** again. If you see the donkey of one who hates you lying under its burden, and you would refrain from helping it, you shall surely **help him** with it. (Ex. 23:4-5).*

The Old Testament taught almost word for word what Jesus does about enemies. Read it for yourself for Proverbs 25:21-22: *"If your enemy is hungry, give him bread to eat; and if he is thirsty, give him water to drink; for so you will heap coals of fire on his head, and the LORD will reward you."*

10. We must keep in mind throughout the sermon that Jesus is not contrasting what He said with what God said through Moses, but rather what "has been said" by the Jewish false teachers for years.

APPENDIX 4

WHY IS UNDERSTANDING THE INFLUENCE AND TEACHING OF THE PHARISEES, ESPECIALLY IN THE BOOK OF MATTHEW, SO IMPORTANT IN THE MDR DISCUSSION?

1. Why is understanding the influence and teaching of the Pharisees, especially in the Book of Matthew, so important in the MDR discussion? What does the teaching of the Jewish leaders have to do with the MDR question? Answer: Practically everything! The teaching of the Scribes and Pharisees are the background for all the teaching Jesus did during His earthly ministry concerning MDR. As a matter of fact, almost everything Jesus taught was correcting the attitudes or exposing the false teachings of the Jewish leaders on this as well as other subjects. The Book of Matthew records the doctrinal/religious "war" between Jesus and the scribes and Pharisees.

2. The entire Book of Matthew, which is the foundation for understanding Jesus' teaching and personal ministry, is filled with references and warnings about their doctrine, practices, and deception. The Book of Matthew begins (Mt. 3:7) and ends (Mt. 23) with a denunciation of

the scribes and Pharisees. The war between the Lord and the Jewish leaders escalated until the leaders had Him crucified.

3. Observe some of the things said about the Jewish leaders in the book of Matthew: They were a brood of snakes (3:7). They did not have the right kind of righteousness (5:20). They criticized Jesus for eating with sinners (9:11). They judged Jesus and His disciples for working on the Sabbath (12:2). They plotted how they might destroy Jesus (12:14). They said Jesus cast out demons by the power of Satan (12:24). They made God's commandments void by their traditions (15:6). They were hypocrites (15:7). Their hearts were far from God (15:8). They taught doctrines of men (15:9). They were offended by Jesus' teaching (15:12). They were blind leaders of blind (15:14). They were sign seekers (16:1). They were wicked and adulterous (16:4). They taught false doctrine (16:12). They tested Jesus (19:3). They tried to trap Jesus (22:15). They bound heavy burdens on other people (23:4). They did not enter the kingdom of God (23:13). They pretended to be very spiritual (23:14-15). They were not merciful (23:23). They were full of sexual uncleanness (23:27). They were full of lawlessness (23:28). They killed and persecuted the people of God (23:34). They paid Judas to betray Jesus (26:14). They sought false witnesses against Jesus (26:59). They said He was worthy of death (26:66). They were envious of Jesus (27:18). They mocked Jesus (27:41). They paid the soldiers to lie about the body of Jesus (28:12-15).

4. It seems to me that, for the most part, **the entire Book of Matthew was directed toward exposing the teachings, attitudes, and actions of the scribes and Pharisees.** Jesus had a purpose for teaching what He did. He did not just pull subjects out of the air to talk about. He taught what He did in many instances because of what His enemies were saying or doing. Note the following point containing examples of things Jesus said in chapters 5-9 of the Book of Matthew and a suggestion for why He said it.

5. Blessed are the poor in spirit (5:3) because the Pharisees were proud (Lk. 18:9-14). Blessed are they that mourn (5:4) because the Pharisees did not mourn over their sins (Lk. 18:9-14). Blessed are the meek

(5:5) because the Pharisees were not meek (23:13). Blessed are those who hunger and thirst after righteousness (5:6) because the Pharisees trusted in themselves that they were already righteous (5:20). Blessed are the merciful (5:7) because the Pharisees omitted mercy (23:23). Blessed are the pure in heart because the Pharisees were impure in their motives (23:28). Blessed are the peacemakers because the Pharisees were persecutors and murderers (23:31). Blessed are those who are per-secuted for righteousness sake (5:10), because that was exactly what the Pharisees did throughout Jesus' ministry (5:12) and would con-tinue to do to His followers (23:34). Whoever breaks one of the least commandments of Moses and teaches others to do so are condemned (5:19) because the Pharisees did that very thing continually (15:6). Do not do your charitable deeds to be seen by others (6:1) because all of the works of the Pharisees were done "to be seen by men" (23:5). Do not pray long prayers like the hypocrites (6:5) because the Pharisees were "hypocrites" who "for a pretense make long prayers" (23:14). Do not fast like the hypocrites who make a show of it (6:16) because the Pharisees did everything for show (23:5). Do not lay up treasures on earth because you cannot serve God and money (6:19-24) because the Pharisees were "lovers of money" (Lk. 16:14) and were full of "extortion" (23:25). Do not judge/condemn/pass judgment on others when you are so obviously sinful yourself (7:1-4) because the Pharisees judged others in this very fashion and neglected their own sins (Lk. 18:9-14). Beware of false prophets who come in sheep's clothing but within are ravenous wolves (7:15) because the Pharisees were hypocrit-ical false teachers and rotten on the inside (23:15, 27). Those who say Lord, Lord, but "who practice lawlessness" will not enter the kingdom of heaven (7:21-23) because the Pharisees were those who "outwardly appear righteous" but were within "full of hypocrisy and lawlessness" (23:28). The sons of the kingdom will be cast into outer darkness (8:12) because the rulers and Pharisees were the guilty ones to whom this lan-guage applies (Lk. 13). Those who are well (righteous) have no need of a physician but those who are sick (9:11-14) because the Pharisees trusted in themselves that they were righteous and did not see them-selves as sin sick (Lk. 18:9-14).

6. The scribes and Pharisees were in "Moses seat" and had approval from Jesus to teach what Moses taught as long as they taught it correctly (Mt. 23:2-3). In other words, Jesus Himself was aware that they were the recognized religious teachers of the day and had influence over His disciples as well as the Jewish people. Therefore, He encourages all to listen to them when they were teaching what Moses actually taught. They had more influence over the thinking of the people than any other person or group at that time. In Matthew 15:12 the Lord's own disciples were worried about offending the Pharisees.

7. The Bible is its own best interpreter. If we allow the Bible to interpret itself then much of the MDR confusion would be cleared up. For example, the attitude of the Jews in the last book of the Old Testament is the same attitude we see "carried over" by the Pharisees in the first book of the New Testament. In Malachi's day they were putting away their Jewish wives in order to marry "pagans" and had gotten involved in worshipping idols (Mal. 2:10-16). During the earthly ministry of Jesus, the Pharisees were also putting away their wives, or causing divorces, in order to marry other men's wives. Plus they were teaching others to do the same thing. I personally believe that this is the reason they asked the questions about divorce and remarriage.

8. In both instances the Jews were dealing treacherously against their wives by putting them away to marry other women, thus committing marital adultery. God hated their sinful doings in Malachi and Jesus exposed what they were doing as sinful in Matthew.

9. The major problem confronted by Jesus was that the Pharisees were "justifying" their sinful conduct. In Luke 16:14-15, Jesus specifically said that the Pharisees were those who "justify yourselves before men." Just three verses later and seemingly "out of the blue" He said that to divorce a wife and marry another is to commit adultery. Why bring up the subject of MDR in this context if they were not doing that very thing? They were obviously teaching that men could divorce their wives for just any cause and marry someone else any time they pleased. As long as she was given "a bill of divorcement" there was nothing wrong with divorcing her and marrying someone else.

10. As we have already mentioned in this book, Jesus did not "destroy" (NKJV) or "abolish" (ESV) or do away with the teaching of the "Law or the Prophets" until its purpose was fulfilled in His death on the cross. If He had made void the teaching of the Law and the Prophets by changing them in the Sermon on the Mount or teaching something different during His earthly ministry, then He could not have fulfilled them. "Do not think that I came to destroy the Law or the Prophets. I did not come to destroy but to fulfill. (Matt. 5:17).

11. Nothing about the teachings in the Law of Moses was changed by Jesus while He was on earth. He did not change or destroy or abolish or cause to pass away the "smallest detail" until it was "all" fulfilled by His death on the cross. *"For assuredly, I say to you, till heaven and earth pass away,* **one jot or one tittle** *will by* **no means pass from the law** *till all is fulfilled."* (Matt. 5:18).

12. Jesus taught in the beginning of His ministry not to "break" or "teach men" to break one of the least of the commandments given by Moses.

> *Whoever therefore* **breaks one** *of the least of these com-mandments, and* **teaches men** *so, shall be called least in the kingdom of heaven; but whoever does and teaches them, he shall be called great in the kingdom of heaven. (Matt. 5:19).*

13. The Law of Moses was "holy, just, and good," (Rom. 7:12), but the weakness was in man's failure to keep it (Heb. 8:8-9) and the inability of sacrifices to take away sins (Heb. 10:1-4). Therefore He "took it out of the way" when He died on the cross (Col. 2:14-17). But it was not fulfilled or taken away until then.

14. It is important to understand and keep in mind that during His earthly ministry Jesus was not changing or correcting the Law of Moses, but rather He was explaining what the Law of Moses actually said and meant.

15. Furthermore, Jesus was showing how the Scribes and Pharisees were corrupting and changing what God had actually said in order to justify their sinful practices. When we keep this in mind then we will know why He said that to divorce a faithful spouse in order to remarry someone else is "committing adultery against her" (Mk. 10:11).

APPENDIX 5

WHAT HAVE OTHERS SAID ABOUT THE "GUILTY PARTY" REMARRYING?

Numerous Christian leaders believed that the guilty party who is put away for fornication can remarry. Among those are:

1. Gus Nichols: *"May the guilty party marry again? I see no way in the world for it to be true that the 'innocent party' may PUT AWAY the 'guilty' party and the 'guilty party' not really be put away. I see no way for the 'innocent party' to have a right to another marriage, but the 'guilty have no such right. If the 'guilty' is REALLY "put away', he is no longer married to the 'innocent party'. How could the 'innocent party' be loosed from the bonds of wedlock, and the 'guilty person' still be tied to the 'innocent'?...It seems to me impossible for the innocent to have the right to another marriage, and the guilty person have no such right.* ("Words of Truth," July 27, 1973, p. 2).

2. J. W. McGarvey: *"Whether it would be adultery to marry a woman who had been put away on account of fornication, is neither affirmed or denied. **No doubt such a woman is at liberty to marry again** if she can, seeing that the bond which bound her to her husband is broken"* (emphasis supplied). (Commentary on Matthew and Mark, p. 165).

3. Bobby Duncan: *"Is he* (a brother) *an enemy to the church because he believes that **the Bible allows the guilty party** in divorce action to **remarry** under certain circumstances* (emphasis supplied) ("Words of Truth," April 13, 1979. It is common knowledge among many of us that Brother Duncan believed that the "guilty party" could remarry in certain circumstances.)

4. Ray Hawk: *"We are informed that when the guilty party, who has committed fornication, is divorced, that the innocent party may remarry. The innocent party is no longer bound to the guilty party. Therefore, since the innocent person is no longer bound to the guilty partner, the innocent party is free to marry again. However, it is **claimed** that the guilty may not remarry because he is still married or bound to the innocent party! **How can that be?** How can one still be married and the other one not married? The simple thing to ask is, "Where is the book, chapter, and verse that so states this teaching?* (emphasis supplied) ("Campbell Street Bulletin," May 26, 1987).

5. Foy E. Wallace, Jr wrote, concerning the permission to divorce in cases involving fornication: *"The treatment of the permissibility of divorce, not a mere separation, but a separation so complete that the marriage tie, or bond of union, is null and void, leaving **both parties** free to **marry again"*** (emphasis supplied) (The Sermon on the Mount and the Civil State, p. 42).

6. G. C. Brewer, one of the most influential preachers from the early to mid-1900s, wrote: *"If the 'innocent party' can marry again, can the 'guilty party' be forgiven of this guilt? If he is forgiven, can he marry again? If not, is he forgiven? How is he forgiven if he is punished for life for his sin?"* (The Truth About Divorce and Remarriage, Weldon Langfield, p. 58).

7. Homer Hailey: *The contention that Genesis 2:18-24 was recognized as law which demanded that the person who takes the wife of another must give her up as demanded by repentance is **disputed in the case of David**.....Surely no one would deny that David repented, yet he was permitted to keep the woman as his wife. Repentance did not demand*

that she be put away or that the two live apart for the remainder of their lives, for she bore him four sons (1 Chron. 3:5). Will not the same God of loving-kindness and tender mercies forgive and blot out sins under a system of grace? Even then it was an act of grace. Would anyone argue that God was more merciful under law than He is under grace? Surely not! (emphasis supplied). (The Divorced and Remarried Who Would Come to God, pp. 72, 73).

APPENDIX 6

WHAT HAVE OTHERS SAID ABOUT DESERTION AND THE RIGHT TO REMARRY

1. Matthew Henry: *"But, though a believing wife or husband should not separate from an unbelieving mate, yet if the unbelieving relative desert the believer, and no means can reconcile to a cohabitation, in such a case a brother or sister is not in bondage (1 Corinthians 7:15), not tied up to the unreasonable humour, and bound servilely to follow or cleave to the malicious deserter, or not bound to live unmarried after all proper means for reconciliation have been tried, at least if the deserter contract another marriage or be guilty of adultery, which was a very easy supposition, because a very common instance among the heathen inhabitants of Corinth. In such a case the deserted person must be free to marry again, and it is granted on all hands. And some think that such a malicious desertion is as much a dissolution of the marriage-covenant as death itself."* (Complete Commentary on the Whole Bible).

2. Macknight: *"Here he declares that the party who was willing to continue the marriage, but who was deserted notwithstanding a reconciliation had been attempted, was at liberty to marry. And his decision is just, because there is no reason why the innocent party, through the*

fault of the guilty party, should be exposed to the danger of committing adultery." (Macknight on the Epistles, Vol. II, p. 107).

3. G. C. Brewer: *"Is the Christian Husband or Wife Who Has Been Maliciously Deserted by an Infidel Partner Free to Marry Again? If not, it would be difficult to see how such 'a brother or a sister is not under bondage in such cases.' If they are not any longer bound to these deserting partners, nor in bondage to them, they certainly are free. If they are not free to marry again, then they are not free from this marriage bondage at all, and are, therefore, still bound. If Paul does not mean that the marriage bondage is broken and does not any longer exist, so far as the Christian is concerned, then his language has no meaning at all. To make it mean something else is to destroy his whole point."* (Contending for the Faith, pp. 100-101)

4. Burton Coffman: *"Some might question whether or not such a brother or sister might remarry; but the view here is that, if not, then the brother or sister would still be in bondage"* (Commentary on 1 Corinthians, p. 104).

5. Jimmy Allen: *"There is not a command or even an implication that he or she is to remain unmarried."* (Commentary on 1 Corinthians, p. 90).

6. R. L. Whiteside: *"If either husband or wife becomes a Christian and the other is so bitter against Christianity as to refuse to live with the believer, the believer is not under bondage in such cases-is completely released from the marriage vows and is as if no marriage had ever taken place. If this be not so, the believer is still under bondage. To me the language means that the brother or sister is as free as if he or she had never been married."* (Reflections, pp. 414, 415).

7. Foy E. Wallace, Jr.: *"Not under bondage, if that does not mean that the believer in these circumstances is free to marry, then it cannot mean anything, for if the one involved is not altogether free the bondage still exists."* (Sermon on the Mount and the Civil State, p. 45).

8. David Lipscomb: *"But if the unbeliever refuses to live with the believer, let him go. The believer is not under bondage in such cases. There is doubt with some as to whether this means the believer is released from the marriage vow and at liberty to marry again, or if it only means he is not under obligation to live with the one who departs. I am inclined to believe the former is the true position."* (Questions Answered by Lipscomb and Sewell, pp. 425, 426).

9. Homer Hailey: *"Jesus made an exception (Matt. 19:3-9), and the Holy Spirit, through Paul, made an exception when he said that the believer is not under bondage (not bound, loosed) in certain cases (1 Cor. 7:15)."* (The Divorced and Remarried Who Would Come to God, p. 39)

10. James D. Bales: Brother Bales wrote a book titled *"Not Under Bondage"* in which he proves without question that the deserted believer is not bound to the deserting unbeliever in any sense and is therefore free to remarry.

11. Neil Lightfoot: *"If the unbeliever deserts or divorces the believer, the believer is released from the marriage bond. The marriage is dissolved. This is the view of the majority of the commentators....and this is the view that I have adopted."* (The Truth about Divorce and Remarriage, Weldon Langfield, p. 71).

12. Alexander Campbell: *"The marriage covenant is broken, and the believer is free. The permission has been granted by the Apostle, and in accordance with the Spirit of God in references to such cases, it seems to me that in all cases of desertion on the side of the unbelieving party, the marriage covenant is made void, and the believing party is to the deserter as though they had never been married..."* (The Truth About Divorce And Remarriage, p. 54).

CPSIA information can be obtained
at www.ICGtesting.com
Printed in the USA
BVHW070238040122
625212BV00005B/605

9 781498 421256